TS-172

PIRANHA S
FACT AND FICTION

John R. Quinn

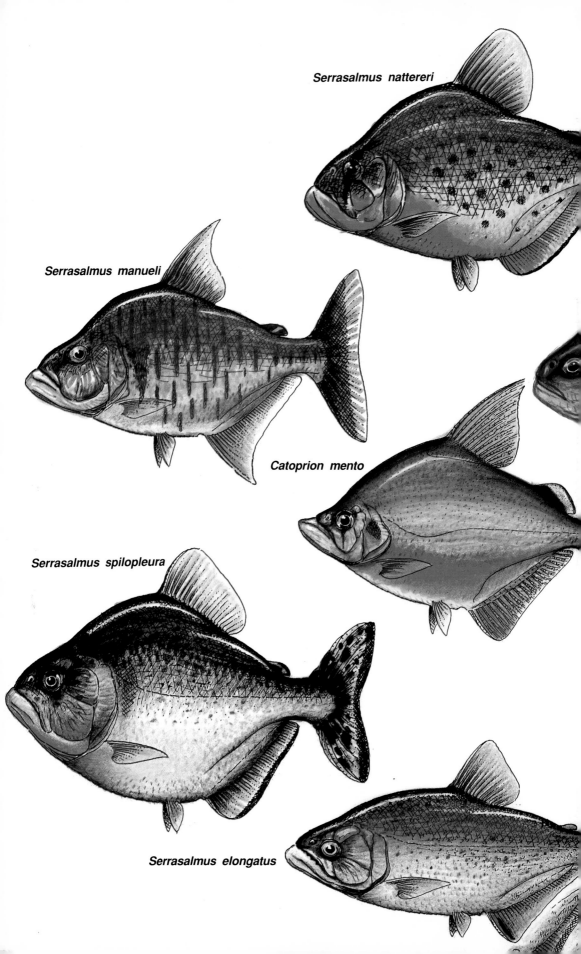

Serrasalmus nattereri

Serrasalmus manueli

Catoprion mento

Serrasalmus spilopleura

Serrasalmus elongatus

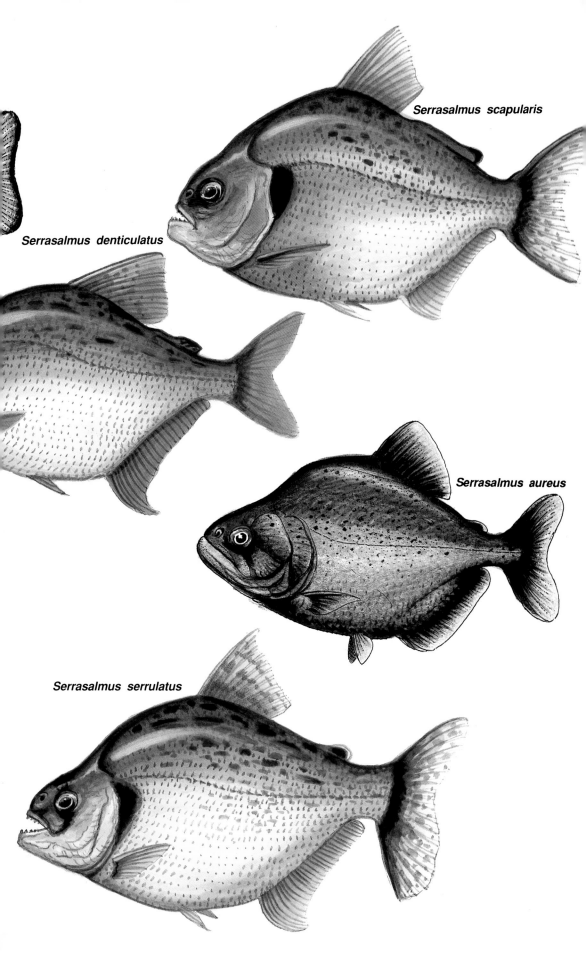

Serrasalmus scapularis

Serrasalmus denticulatus

Serrasalmus aureus

Serrasalmus serrulatus

PHOTO AND ARTISTIC CREDITS

Dr. Herbert R. Axelrod, Burkhard Kahl, H. Bleher, A. Fernandez-Yepez, Heinrich Stolz, Harald Schultz, Hans-Joachim Richter, K. Knaack, Andrew Prendimano, INPA, Michael Gilroy, I. Sazima, Aquarium Bologna, D. Conkel, Aaron Norman, Hiroshi Azuma, Jiri Palicka, J.J. van Duinen, Dr. Leo G. Nico, Dr. Donald Taphorn and John R. Quinn.

Serrasalmus antoni collected by Dr. Herbert R. Axelrod in the Rio Aguaro in Venezuela in 1971. The fish was described by Dr. A. Fernandez-Yepez, whose face is in the background. Photo by Dr. Herbert R. Axelrod.

PIRANHAS
FACT AND FICTION

John R. Quinn

For Ray Hamlin, nephew and first-rate fishkeeper.

Distributed in the UNITED STATES by T.F.H. Publications, Inc., One
T.F.H. Plaza, Neptune City, NJ 07753; in CANADA to the Pet Trade by H
& L Pet Supplies Inc., 27 Kingston Crescent, Kitchener, Ontario N2B 2T6;
Rolf C. Hagen Ltd., 3225 Sartelon Street, Montreal 382 Quebec; in
CANADA to the Book Trade by Macmillan of Canada (A Division of Canada
Publishing Corporation), 164 Commander Boulevard, Agincourt, Ontario
M1S 3C7; in ENGLAND by T.F.H. Publications, PO Box 15, Waterlooville
PO7 6BQ; in AUSTRALIA AND THE SOUTH PACIFIC by T.F.H. (Austra-
lia) Pty. Ltd., Box 149, Brookvale 2100 N.S.W., Australia; in NEW ZEAL-
AND by Ross Haines & Son, Ltd., 82 D Elizabeth Knox Place, Panmure,
Auckland, New Zealand; in the PHILIPPINES by Bio-Research, 5 Lippay
Street, San Lorenzo Village, Makati, Rizal; in SOUTH AFRICA by Multipet
Pty. Ltd., P.O. Box 35347, Northway, 4065, South Africa. Published by
T.F.H. Publications, Inc. Manufactured in the United States of America by
T.F.H. Publications, Inc.

TABLE OF CONTENTS

Introduction

WHY KEEP PIRANHAS?

There's no doubt that much of the popularity of the piranha as an aquarium fish today stems from the creature's undeniable aura of mystery and menace. The piranha is a predator *par excellence,* and for many hobbyists it is by far this aspect of the piranha's behavior and adaptation that has the greatest appeal. While in fact a captive piranha, especially a large individual, must be treated with healthy respect and handled with no small degree of caution, much of the piranha's reputation as a mindless, bloodthirsty killer has been embellished and exaggerated over the years, overblown so that the living fish has been transformed into something resembling pure myth and legend, and a terrifying one at that!

The great majority of people gazing at a flock of little piranhas milling about in a petshop tank are convinced that they would instantly lose a finger should they so much as dip that digit in the tank for a second! This persistent piranha perception on the part

of the public has been fostered for the most part by many years of some rather sensational prose by a considerable host of writers, some of them in a position of firsthand, practical knowledge, but many others spouting so much piscine baloney.

Theodore Roosevelt wrote extensively on the piranha, being obviously impressed with both the physical appearance and the reputation of the fish he encountered during his several Amazon expeditions in the early years of this Century. A typical account penned by the intrepid statesman/explorer relates how piranhas ". . . are the most fercocious fish in the world. Even the most formidable fish, the sharks or the barracudas, usually attack things much smaller than themselves. But the piranhas habitually attack things much larger than themselves. They will snap a finger off a hand incautiously trailed in the water; they mutilate swimmers—in every river town in Paraguay there are

A great souvenir from Brazil is a preserved piranha with a glass eye and its lips cut away to show the teeth. They are on sale in every curio shop along the Amazon and at Brazilian airports. Photo by Dr. Herbert R. Axelrod.

men who have been mutilated; they will rend and devour alive any wounded man or beast; for blood in the water excites them to madness   . . ."

Dr. Herbert R. Axelrod, the famous collector of South American fish, was written up in *Sports Illustrated* and *Time* magazines when he told the world on the Johnny Carson Television Show that he regularly swims with piranhas and is not afraid of them in any river in South America.

Time magazine challenged him to swim with piranhas in Brazil. Down the Amazon went Axelrod with a *Time* reporter. At the given place, Axelrod stripped to his barest necessities and took a short fishing rod about 40 inches long. On the end was a piece of wire and a hook with stale meat on it. He jumped into the water. It was about 4 feet deep. He dropped the baited hook into the water right near him, and within a minute pulled in an 8-inch long piranha. After ten piranhas were caught the myth of the dangerous piranha was forever broken and Teddy Roosevelt's public relations gimmick was exposed for what it was.

Later, on a similar trip with the German fish photographer Hans-Joachim Richter, Dr. Axelrod did the same thing. The action was duplicated by Richter with Axelrod photographing it. Piranhas are not dangerous to living people in running water. They are dangerous in lakes which may be drying out and in which all the food fishes have already been eaten and the piranhas are starving.

A hard literary act to follow, to be sure, and separating piranha fact from fiction will be just one of the aims of this book.

For the average hobbyist, the introduction to the living, breathing piranha often arrives as he or she stands before that display tank in a local petshop and gazes with dubious awe at what appear to be little more than small, silvery, somewhat large-mouthed and obviously nervous characins—hardly more impressive than any one of the smaller tetras so popular in the hobby. The tank is clearly labelled **"piranha",** but the fish therein look anything but dangerous, and the neophyte is often left to wonder just what all the fuss over piranhas is about. Most of the piranhas sold in the retail market today are of the red-bellied species *(Serrasalmus nattereri)* and the great majority of these are one-to-three-inch juveniles

Even small piranhas have razor-sharp, scissors-like teeth.

that were collected in the wild. Although adorned with dusky spots and reddish fins and looking for all the world like deep-bodied, big-eyed tetras, a closer look at the half-pint piranhas in the dealer's tank will quickly reveal their true identity; although the legendary teeth are often not visible in a young piranha, the aggressive, underslung jaw leaves little doubt in the mind of the observer that this is a predator, and an efficient one at that. And like all animals, little piranhas have the habit of sooner or later turning into big piranhas.

Few piranha buyers today are naive or uninformed enough to simply purchase one and blithely introduce the fish into a community tank filled with potential victims. Most know fully well what they've purchased. But there is more to piranha-keeping, much more, than the notion that these fishes are little more than exotic, finned executioners whose primary purpose in an aquarium is to shred an endless procession of feeder goldfish for the amusement of houseguests. Piranhas are superbly adapted, beautiful creatures with a natural history that will both amaze and educate the serious aquarist seeking to get the most out of the hobby. Given the right care and attention to requirements, piranhas will co-exist with each other in the captive environment and conduct their affairs in a manner closely duplicating that of the wild state, up to and including spawning.

The notion of the piranha as an aquarium fish, a "pet," if you will, was almost unknown up until about 20 years ago. Prior to that time, the aquarium hobby itself was still pretty much in the "bread and butter" stage. The great majority of the fishes available to and thus kept by casual hobbyists were farm-raised livebearers and the growing array of peaceful (in other words, *harmless)* species collected in the tropics. Piranhas were generally considered too exotic and difficult to both ship and care for, as well as potentially dangerous and best left to zoos and public aquariums. To a degree, they are indeed all of these things, but with the advent of much more sophisticated aquarium hardware in recent years plus the great increase in the body of knowledge of these fishes and their environmental requirements, the successful keeping of any of the various piranha species in the home aquarium is no longer an impossible dream. All it requires is a lively interest in the fish for its own unique and fascinating attributes, careful attention to its needs, and the willingness to view your piranha-keeping experience as an education in one of nature's most fascinating and misunderstood creatures.

So if you're that special person, that adventurous hobbyist willing to "look beyond the legend" and search for the real piranha, to create a microcosm of this beautiful characin and its unique tropical habitat in the home, and to perhaps try your hand at spawning these fascinating fishes, this book is for you, and we invite you to read on!

Most of the small red-bellied piranhas look alike.

Piranhas can be friend or foe. Most of their reputation is based upon distortions of the truth by the late great President Theodore Roosevelt. Piranhas are a necessity in jungle waters and none of the local inhabitants are afraid of them *unless the water is a small lake which is drying out and in which the piranhas have eaten all the other fishes.*

The Piranha in Fact and Fancy

The great majority of the world's fishes—both living and extinct—were and are predators. That is, they secure nourishment by attacking and eating other animals, principally other fishes. True, there are many fishes that are primarily **vegetarian,** but these are definitely in the minority—most fishes are **carnivores.** When people think of meat-eating fishes, especially those whose means of securing their meals could conceivably present them as a threat to people who find themselves in the fishes present habitat—the water— they conjure up images of three piscine groups: the sharks, the barracudas, and the piranhas. And not always in that order.

Piranhas are active, attractive fishes that more than most characins, seem to exhibit more than the usual amount of fish intelligence, which isn't much in most cases. In nature, the outwitting and securing of prey always demands more from a fish than the less complex strategy of simply avoiding becoming prey. The strategy usually consists of varying approaches to the flight response, protective mimicry, or simply laying low and not moving a muscle. Like any other predator, the piranha must be able to discern whether a potential prey animal is approachable and catchable and then maneuver to within effective striking distance. It must also develop a sense as to where its preferred prey species are likely to be at the greatest disadvantage—as in very swift water or near tangles of vegetation—and seek them out in such situations, often in ambush. Although piranhas often attack *en masse* when a victim of any size is assaulted, they are quite capable of playing the lone wolf and often cruise alone in search of food, employing stealth and something approaching guile when sighting a school of likely prospects.

These abilities on the part of the piranha, plus its robust, no-nonsense appearance and demeanor, have combined in recent years to make the fish an endless source of fascination to humans, even those who haven't the slightest interest in keeping one in a home aquarium.

Although piranhas were virtually unknown in the collective Western consciousness until the early years of this Century (they were first *popularly*—as opposed to *scientifically*— described by the explorer Alexander von Humboldt at about 1800), the group quickly became the subject of a vast volume of literature, much of it based on the fish's legendary ferocity and perceived threat to man. Many and colorful were the accounts—still regarded as fact today—of man or beast skeletonized within seconds by a swarm of berserk piranhas. Typical of the genre is the following account, written by an early ichthyologist purporting to be intimately familiar with the piranha in its home turf: *"Normally the piranha is a calm fish, but when a victim appears, it appears to go berserk, and what compels it is not hunger alone. Long after the fish have eaten their fill, they continue with their furious attacks until not even the tiniest shred of flesh is* *left; the remains pile up on the bottom of the river until the current sweeps them away. No living creature escapes their attention, not even one of their own genus, and it is impossible to keep more than one of these fish in one and the same aquarium."* The same writer went on to note that *"death caused by the shark or the barracuda tends to be quick, and, as compared with death by the piranha, can virtually be described as merciful."*

Humboldt himself, in his log of his adventures along the Apure River, had this to say about the piranha: *"On the morning of the 3rd of April our Indians caught with hook the fish known in the country by the name of* **caribe,** meaning **'cannibal,'** *because no other fish has such a thirst for blood. It attacks bathers and swimmers, from whom it often bites away considerable pieces of flesh. The Indians dread these caribes extremely. Several of them showed us the scars of deep wounds in the calf of the leg and in the thigh made by these little animals. They swim at the bottom of rivers; but if a few drops of blood be shed on the water, they rise by the thousands to the surface, so that if a person be only slightly bitten, it is difficult for him to get out of*

This piranha lost its nose after a pre-spawning battle. Piranhas heal in an amazingly short time.

the water without receiving a severe wound. When we reflect on the numbers of these fish, the largest and most voracious of which are only four or five inches long, on the triangular form of their sharp and cutting teeth, and on the amplitude of their retractile mouths, we need not be surprised at the fear which

considered one of the greatest scourges of those climates in which the sting of the mosquitoies and the general irritation of the skin render the use of baths so neccesary."

It can be seen from the above account, presumably written "on the scene" though sprinkled with several inaccuracies, that the impression was often deliberately created, both in the print and motion picture media, that any person entering the piranha's habitat would at once be attacked and

Serrasalmus nattereri. This old fellow swims around with his teeth flashing. This characteristic is found only in older fish. Photo by Hans-Joachim Richter.

the caribe excites in the inhabitants of the banks of the Apure and Orinoco.

"In places where the river was very limpid, where not a fish appeared, we threw into the water little morsels of raw flesh, and in a few minutes a perfect cloud of caribes came to dispute their prey. . . . As no one dares to bathe where it is found, it may be

quickly reduced to shredded clothing and bones within minutes by the nearest school of these malevolent creatures. That a piranha can attack, dispatch, and eat its prey within seconds, depending on its size, there is no doubt. But just where in all the tangled verbiage on the fish's diet, and its means of securing it, does sensationalism and fiction take leave of common sense and fact?

A mere four, possibly five species of piranha—all of them of the genus *Serrasalmus*—are considered potentially dangerous to humans entering their habitat. These are: *S. piraya, S. nattereri, S. niger, S. rhombeus*, and *S. eigenmanni*. These are powerful, robust species, generally fishes of rare or local distribution and typified by the subgenus *Pristobrycon*, which includes *Serrasalmus aureus, S. serrulatus*, and *S. emarginatus*, among others.

To get a handle on the nature of the threat any given species of piranha will pose to a human being in the wild, one must first learn something

Serrasalmus nattereri. **Photo by Heinrich Stolz.**

fishes showing the blunt, convex head profile and strongly underslung jaw of the effective slashing-and-cutting predator. The non-aggressive species, generally displaying an elongate, narrow-headed profile characteristic of the schooling, fish-eating predator, are collectively known as *pirambebas*. In between are the "marginal" about the fish's natural prey. Like sharks, which may also attack people and other terrestrial animals they might encounter in their habitat, the principal food of the piranha in nature is other fishes, and usually smaller ones. The attacking and devouring of warm-blooded animals must be considered the exception rather than the rule in piranha feeding behavior.

It would stand to reason that any predator will instinctively select the prey item that it can most easily overpower and which it readily recognizes as food, rather than animals which are larger, more powerful, or outside its inherited experience as belonging in the blood or other body fluids present in the water. As with the marine sharks and the voracious bluefish, piranhas quickly become excited when such substances enter the water and at once begin the characteristic, agitated "sweeping" behavior in an attempt to locate the source of food.

Note the bulldog face with the rounded forehead on this *Serrasalmus piraya*. The Germans call piranhas pirayas. Photo by J.J. van Duinen.

habitat and being a normal source of nourishment. Although some piranha species are omnivorous and will eat certain fruits that may drop into the water from streamside vegetation, the great majority are attracted to living prey—almost always other fishes—either by its actions or through the scent of

As in most other fishes, the sense of smell is very highly developed in piranhas, enabling them to quickly locate the source of blood or bodily fluids, even in the murkiest water. German aquarist Wolfgang Schulte tested the extent of the olfactory powers of the piranha in experiments

*Serrasalmus
piraya*
photographed
by Burkhard
Kahl.

Large piranhas like this one must be well fed to get along with others. This fish was photographed by Burkhard Kahl in an aquarium in Germany.

conducted with a 10-inch specimen he kept in a 52-gallon aquarium. Schulte noted that *"a single drop of blood or meat juice placed in the tank was enough to cause (the fish) to become visibly* diffused scent of blood in the water can attract a great number of piranhas in a very short time!

It should be noted that not all fishes singled out as a potential meal by a piranha

agitated. Several drops induced the piranha to swim toward the supposed prey. This was always followed by a phase of swimming about at great speed. Pieces of meat lying on the bottom were invariably approached and picked up in a very purposeful manner, and bits of food hidden among dense vegetation were always found very quickly." Given such sensitive olfactory acuity, it is no small wonder that even a invariably end up as fodder for the predator. Recent research conducted in the natural habitat has shown that, in addition to the well-known color and form mimicry practiced by the various pacus, other fishes, particularly cichlids, have developed specific defensive behaviors against piranha attack. Included are tail protecting, alert watching, and direct confrontational actions on the part of the victim,

Compare the profile of the face of this *Serrasalmus striolatus* with the fish on the facing page. Photo by INPA.

Serrasalmus niger collected by Dr. Axelrod in the Rio Trombetas. The fish was 15 inches long! Photo by Dr. Martin Brittan.

which often caused the attacking piranha to back off and abort the assault. There is no doubt that piranhas have a powerful effect on the respective fish communities in which they live and on habitat use by other species that share it with them.

Sound waves travel four to five times faster in water than they do in the atmosphere, hence it would stand to reason that the hearing of the piranha is at least as acute as in other bony fishes. Hearing and the sense of balance are contained within the labyrinth in the head of the fish. All fishes produce low-frequency vibrations when swimming in a normal fashion, and the change in frequency resulting from the struggles of an injured or sick fish would certainly prove a strong attractant to every piranha in the vicinity. For this reason, piranhas, like the marine sharks, are drawn by the movements of an injured animal and may, in times of drought when the fish are concentrated in smaller, shrinking bodies of water and very hungry, attack human swimmers.

Piranhas are usually much more dangerous to man out of the water than in it and the great majority of bite injuries occur on shore or in boats during the course of fishing activity. These fishes fight vigorously when hooked and thrash actively about when landed, accompanied by a fast shivering action of the head and much jaw-snapping. Given the powerful jaw muscles and more than adequate teeth, a piranha that connects with any part of the human anatomy, if carelessly handled, can easily clip a neat wad of flesh from a hand or arm, and, given the right (or wrong) set of circumstances, a large specimen could easily sever a finger.

The response on the part of a captive piranha to the sudden appearance of a human hand in its tank in the vast majority of cases consists of the flight reaction—but there can be exceptions to this. Unless the fish are very hungry, they will almost never actively investigate the object or attack the aquarist reaching into their quarters, but open sores or bleeding wounds are a foolish invitation to trouble. Sudden moves should also be avoided; the rearrangement of plants and other artifacts in the tank should be done with deliberation and care, with the use of tongs or planting sticks strongly advised, in a tank containing large piranhas, no matter how long you've had them or how "tame" they

A *Crenicichla lepidota* defends itself against a piranha attack by a direct eyeball-to-eyeball confrontation.

A *Crenicichla lepidota* defends its tail against a scale-eating *Serrasalmus spilopleura* by laying it flat against the bottom.

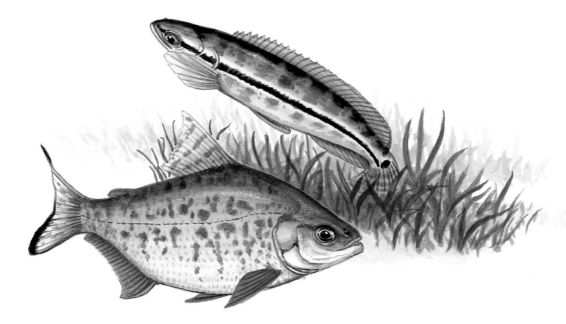

A piranha, *Serrasalmus spilopleura* sneaking up on a feeding cichlid to bite off a bit of its tail.

A group of cichlids, *Aequidens*, form a military-like defense against an attack by a piranha. Drawings by the author.

Serrasalmus nattereri. Photo by Burkhard Kahl.

seem to be! Any hand motion that serves to corner or otherwise indicate an impending threat to a piranha seeking to avoid contact with its owner may well have the expected result. The word to the wise in piranha keeping is: a mishandled piranha, even a small one, has the potential to do some damage and inflict a nasty wound, so treat with respect!

It should be noted that piranhas are really no more predatory than most carnivorous fishes (and the great majority of the world's living fishes are indeed carnivores), but given their highly social nature and method of attacking en masse, plus their formidable, razor-sharp teeth, common sense and caution should be employed when handling or coming in contact with the fish in captivity. Whenever a potentially dangerous predatory animal is confined in an unnatural environment—such as a cage or an aquarium—the rules of the game quickly change, as any zoo person well knows! Respect the nature of the beast, or don't keep large piranhas—it's as simple as that.

The true nature of the danger posed by piranhas in

prefer to avoid them because of the damage they can do to nets, many rural people eat piranhas. They are not too bony and the flavor is similar to that of their vegetarian cousins, the pacus. So if we

Serrasalmus spilopleura. Photo from INPA.

their natural environment may be summed up in the words of ichtyologists Leo G. Nico and Donald C. Taphorn, who wrote in *Tropical Fish Hobbyist* : "Humans catch prianhas frequently and though commercial fishermen

were keeping score, the piranhas could justifiably claim that 'human infested' shores are the most dangerous in the world—for in the end, we bite them a lot more than they bite us."

The Nature of the Name

Before the First World War, hardly anyone outside of South America had heard of the word piranha nor of the fearsome creature it was attached to. Today, the word is found in all English language dictionaries and virtually everybody, even those who wouldn't know an oscar from an airstone, at least knows what a piranha is, if little beyond that.

The name itself, which is the one in the widest use today but by no means the only label applied to the fish, comes from the widespread South American Indian language called "Tupi-Guarani." The exact meaning is unclear, but the more plausible root might be found in the fact that "pira"means fish in the Lingua Geral (General Tongue), or patois, spoken nearly throughout Brazil. In the same language, the word for tooth is variously given as "ranha," "tanha," or "sanha," leaving us with the literal translation of "fish-tooth," or, more reasonably,

"toothed-fish." This makes complete sense, given the nature of the beast, but it might be worth relating that in the convoluted ways of most of the world's languages and dialects, the word "piranha" also means simply common, everyday household scissors along many sections of the Amazon. But that definition makes sense, too, when you think about it.

The word piranha is correctly pronounced "pee-rahn-yah"—not "peranna" as is often the case throughout most of the English-speaking world. The accent is on the "rahn," and the "r" rolled, which is the way anyone speaking Spanish or Portuguese in Brazil would say it.

Although the word "piranha" is the one best known to most people outside South America and usually applied to all piranha species, regardless of type and perceived degree of danger to man, the people who live with the fish are considerably more

This *Serrasalmus striolatus* was collected in the Rio Marmelos (Rio Madeira system) by Dr. Herbert R. Axelrod. He also photographed it. This fish is infested with parasites which are harmless to the host and other fishes in the same tank.

discriminating and selective in their choice of labels for the many kinds of piranhas they are familiar with. In Brazil, the word is applied only to those species deemed dangerous to man—those of the genus *Serrasalmus*—the others being called, in general, "pirambebas," or

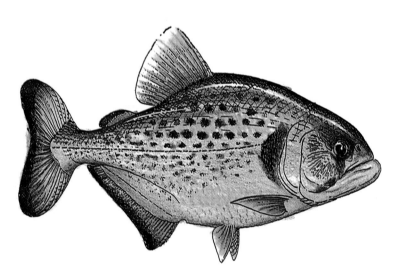

"pirampebas." This word has its roots in the Tupi words "piranha" and "peba," meaning "flat," an apt combination and descriptive term, as most of the inoffensive species of *Serrasalmus* are strongly compressed both in head and body, while the more aggressive species—the true "piranhas"—show a much more robust form.

In much of Spanish-speaking Venezuela, the common, larger, more dangerous species of piranhas are referred to as "Caribes" (pronounced "car-ree-bays"). This name originated with the Caribes, a warlike tribe of South American Indians which eventually spread throughout the West Indies, ruthlessly subjugating and generally terrorizing the more gentle tribes who preceded them as they went. The Caribes were numerous, adventuresome, and very fierce, so the application of their name to a group of equally pugnacious fishes is quite apt.

To round out the roster of local names that have been attached to the piranha in one place or another throughout the broad range of the group, we might add: "palometa" in Bolivia; "umati" in the Orinoco Basin; "panya" in Amazonian Peru; and "pirai" in the Guianas.

The Business End
—The Piranha's Teeth

A placid, strictly vegetarian piranha doesn't exist, at least among the true piranhas, and indeed, the reputation of this fish would never have ever gotten off the ground if it were not for those all-important component parts of its anatomy—its teeth. A brief discussion of this aspect of the piranhas might serve to provide the hobbyist with the physical nature of any threat to life and limb should a captive piranha be related to or handled injudiciously.

Unlike the teeth of the sharks, the dentition of the piranhas is not designed for lacerating, crushing, mangling, or holding prey; they are more implements for snipping, or clipping neat sections of flesh from an organism, rendering the prey into small, bite-sized, swallowable pieces. Unlike the teeth of sharks, which are arranged in rows that move up and succeed each other on "the front line" as wear or damage removes their effectiveness, piranha teeth are set in the short, broad jaws in a single row. These are sharper than sharks' teeth and their mechanics remind one of the design and operation of a bear trap, in that when the piranha's jaws snap shut, the points of the teeth in the upper row fit neatly into the notches of those in the lower row. Ichthyologist George S. Myers has said that "the

Piranhas' teeth are sharp and pointed and the top teeth mesh with the bottom teeth like a bear trap.

power of the jaw muscles is such that there is scarcely any piranhas is not difficult to visualize!

The strength and power of the piranha's bite both originate and can be seen in the extremely deep and powerful lower jaw of the more dangerous species. The muscle mass and their attachments are very dense and provide the fish with the legendary cutting power synonymous with its name. In the piranha's natural habitat, Amazonian and Guianan Indians have from prehistoric times to the present day used piranha teeth as ready implements to cut bark, thongs, hair, wood, or anything else remotely cutable. All of this should serve as fair warning to any hobbyist tempted to take foolish liberties with his or her captive specimens!

Piranhas have their own natural enemies...Crocodiles and aquatic mammals like River Dolphin. As these animals disappear, the piranhas breed out of control!

Serrasalmus antoni was described by Fernandez-Yepez in 1965. This *S. antoni* was collected by Dr. Axelrod, who cut away the lips for this photograph.

Facing page: The pugnacious aspect of *Serrasalmus nattereri* is captured well in this view.

living substance save the hardest ironwood that will not be clipped off." Indeed, although the mouth of even a large piranha is relatively small in relation to the overall size of the fish, the average bite would neatly excise a piece of flesh the size of a large olive. That may not seem like much of a mouthful, but when one considers the piranha's rapid-fire method of snap, swallow, and return for more, the idea of a prey animal disappearing within minutes under the combined assault of a large school of

Serrasalmus elongatus

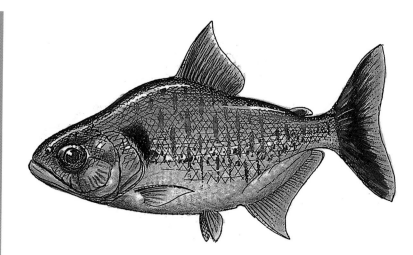

Serrasalmus fernandezi

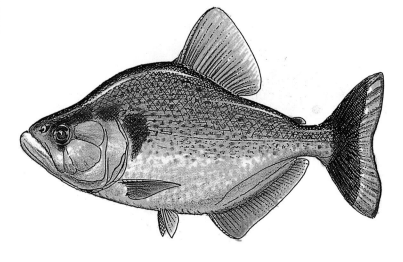

Serrasalmus nalseni

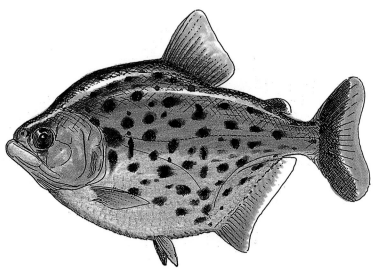

Rogue's Gallery— The Species

Piranhas are characins, just as the popular and considerably more placid tetras are, and as such they possess that characteristic fleshy adipose fin on the caudal peduncle. The taxonomy of the piranha group has historically been a confusing and essentially unsettled affair and its final determination is far from settled even today. Many current species have been discribed solely on the basis of color and body form, factors that often change radically as the fish grows and matures, so the validity of some species has to be viewed with no small degree of caution. In the latest determination piranhas are members of the order Cypriniformes, suborder Characoidei. There are 14 families in this suborder, one of them being the family Serrasalmidae, which contains the piranhas. The subfamily Serrasalminae is comprised solely of the true piranhas of the genus *Serrasalmus*, which, with the exception of the scale-eating wimple piranhas (*Catoprion* species), are by far the species most often kept in aquaria by hobbyists. In all, there are about 35 species of piranha in South America, with a dozen or so occurring in the Orinoco Basin. Although the taxonomy of the piranhas remains unsettled, the recognized major classification of the group today is as follows:

Class: Osteichthys, the bony fishes.
Superorder: Teleostei, the true bony fishes.
Order: Cypriniformes, the carp-like fishes.
Suborder: Characoidei, the characins.
Family: Serrasalmidae, including the genus *Serrasalmus.*
Subfamily: Serrasalminae, piranha-like fishes.
Genus: *Serrasalmus,* with

4 subgenera and more than 20 species.

Subgenus *Pygopristis:*

Serrasalmus denticulatus, Caribe Palometa: from the Guianas and lower Amazon; a nonaggressive species seldom seen in the hobby. Reaches a length of about 8 inches.

Subgenus *Pristobrycon:*

Serrasalmus aureus, Caribe Dorado: from Brazil and possibly the Caquiare region of Venezuela; one of the two so-called "gold piranhas," this fish is a large (13 inches) species that occasionally appears in the aquarium hobby, mostly in larger sizes and commanding high prices. The adult is an olivaceous and gold creature with a very attractive iridescence. The gold piranha is not considered a species dangerous to man.

Serrasalmus gibbus, the yellow, or gold piranha: from the Amazon and tributaries and Peru. An aggressive species that cannot be maintained with any other fishes except, possibly, for large catfishes. Reaches the length of 8 to 12 inches in the wild, though most aquarium specimens are smaller. The color is distinctive: steel-blue to violet on the back, shading to a beautiful deep yellow or gold on the sides and belly. There are many small, iridescent scales on the sides.

Serrasalmus emarginatus, from Suriname; a nonaggressive species uncommon in the aquarium

Serrasalmus denticulatus

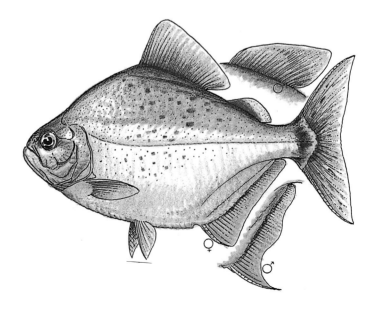

hobby. Unlike many other piranha species, which are quite social and tend to form schools, this fish is reportedly more solitary in nature though it will unobtrusively join schools of other larger characins and even other

species is one of the largest at an adult length of between 14 and 16 inches. Not often seen in the aquarium hobby.

Serrasalmus scapularis, Caribe capa Caballo: from Rio Essequibo, Guyana;

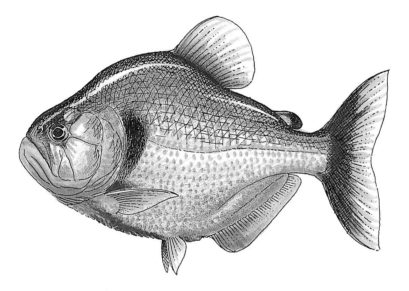

Serrasalmus scapularis

piranhas in order to stalk and attack them. Their natural diet consists primarily of the fins and scales of its victims and the young of this species have been observed removing parasites from adult *S. nattereri*, much in the manner of the marine cleaner wrassel.

Serrasalmus serrulatus; The Amazon, and the Rio Atacavi, Venezuela. Although not considered one of the dangerous piranhas, this

probably a synonym; uncommon in the hobby.

Serrasalmus gymnogenys: Suriname and the lower Amazon region;

Serrasalmus striolatus; from Rio Para and Rio Tapanohony, Guyana;

Serrasalmus calmoni; the dusky piranha: a large, though not very colorful species, this fish is infrequently offered in the aquarium hobby as it is of very local distribution. Reaches the length of about 9 inches and is characterized by the reddish anal fin and dark humeral (shoulder) spot.

Serrasalmus bilineatus: from Rio Aruca, Guyana.

Serrasalmus coccogenis: from Venezuela.

circumstances. Non-breeding adults are a steel blue to olivaceous above, fading to a bright silvery on the sides and white on the belly. Breeding adults generally become very dark, almost black, with rosy and purplish overtones.

Serrasalmus elongatus; the pike piranha: from the Orinoco basin though Dr. Axelrod collected them in a

Serrasalmus elongatus was originally described by Dr. Kner in 1860. This specimen was collected in 1976 by Dr. Axelrod in the shallow (less than 6 feet deep) Lake Las Pupunhas off the Rio Madeira of Brazil. Photo by Dr. Axelrod.

Subgenus *Serrasalmus*:

Serrasalmus eigenmanni; pinche piranha, Caribe Lagunero: from Rio Essequibo, Rio Potaro, Guyana; although this fish has the rather elongated body shape and longer snout of the typical "pirambeba," it is considered an aggressive species known to attack people under certain

lake near Humaita, on the Rio Madeira in Brazil, 2000 miles away!. This is one of the more slim species and is primarily an eater of the fins and scales of larger fishes as well as entire smaller fishes. Non-breeding adults and juveniles are a rather plain silvery color. The pike piranha is not considered dangerous to man.

Serrasalmus rhombeus; Caribe Amarillo, the white piranha. Widely distributed in the Amazon and Orinoco regions and throughout Guyana region. Possibly

Serrasalmus hollandi; Holland's piranha: from the Amazon region, though exact range not determined; a smaller species (6 inches) that is generally non-aggressive

Serrasalmus hollandi collected and photographed by Dr. Axelrod in the Rio Aguaro, Venezuela.

synonymous with *S. niger*. A large (14 to 18 inches), aggressive species suspected in attacks on man. The young are slim, active creatures that show the "typical" juvenile pattern of dark speckles and spots, but as they grow, the fish become more robust and high-backed, and the color darkens to a grayish-brown or even black. The black edging to the anal and caudal fins is distinctive of this species.

and not considered dangerous to man. A slim, laterally compressed fish characterized by its high-backed profile and prominent blackish shoulder spot; the caudal fin is transparent with a blackish base. This fish darkens with age, becoming almost black at maturity and especially so when spawning.

Serrasalmus spilopleura; Caribe Cachamero: from the

Amazon region as far as the La Plata plain, Orinoco region, and the Lago del Guarico, Venezuela; moderately aggressive. This species has a very strongly compressed body and an elongate head with an underslung jaw. It reaches the length of between 10 and 12 in attacks on man, though in many areas throughout their range they are relatively uncommon and do not molest swimmers. The black piranha is a moderately large species, reaching the adult length of 14 inches. The body is strongly compressed laterally and displays a prominent, hump-

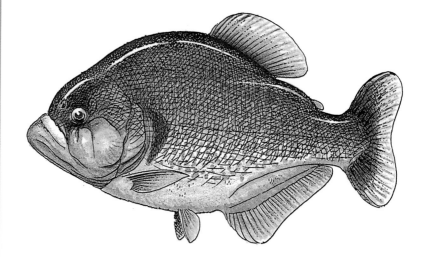

Serrasalmus niger.

inches. Adults usually have bright red eyes. Not considered dangerous, though this fish is quite capable of inflicting a savage bite. In nature it is primarily a fin and scale eater and as such cannot be kept with any other species, even the larger piranha species, upon which it may prey.

Serrasalmus niger, the black piranha: the Guianas; an aggressive species implicated

backed profile. Although this fish is sometimes available in the aquarium hobby, it can be difficult to maintain, even in a single-species tank, due to its aggressive nature; adults can be extremely touchy and unpredictable, even in larger tanks.

Serrasalmus piraya: from the lower Amazon region and the Rio São Francisco, Brazil; perhaps the most aggressive species in the wild state. This is the largest of the piranhas, reaching the length of about 20 inches at maturity; individuals two feet long have been reported, though not verified. It has been implicated in attacks on man. The fish has the large rounded head and underslung mouth characteristic of the more

larger size in the full adult (not definitive) and the tufted, fibrous adipose fin characteristic of *S. piraya*.

S. piraya is, for obvious reasons, ideally kept only in large display tanks, for it is a fast-growing fish and requires plenty of room if there is to be

Serrasalmus piraya. Photo by Burkhard Kahl.

aggressive species, and the forehead is strongly convex. Adults of this species can be difficult to distinguish from the red-bellied piranha, the principal means being the

any peace at all when more than two or three are housed together. It should be offered larger feeder fishes (such as shiners or goldfish) as well as nightcrawlers and strips of

fish or lean beef. This species has not yet been spawned in captivity.

Serrasalmus nattereri, red-bellied piranha; caribe: very widely distributed throughout the Amazon and Orinoco regions, the Guianas, and the Rio Paraguay and Rio Parana. This species is by far the most common in the hobby and usually readily available to the aquarist through retail aquarium stores. It is not an exceptionally large species, as piranhas go, reaching the adult length of between 7 and 10 inches, considerably smaller than the very similar *S. piraya*. The adults of both species are olive-brownish above, silvery on the sides and usually have a reddish flush on the throat and abdomen; *S. piraya*, however, generally displays a much brighter scale iridescence on the flanks.

The red-bellied piranha is considered one of the more dangerous species within its range and is doubtless the source of most of the reported piranha attacks on humans. In nature it is primarily a fish eater, so live fishes are the preferred food in aquaria, although the species will accept most larger live foods, including earthworms, and chunks of cut fish or lean beef.

Serrasalmus nigricans: from the Amazon and Orinoco regions; considered aggressive. This is a medium-sized piranha, mature at about 10 inches. It is similar in form to *S. nattereri* but has a smaller head and jaw structure and lacks the red color in either body or fins. The tail is virtually truncate in adult specimens, showing little or no notch. In all ages, the anal and caudal fins have a dark margin, which contrasts strongly with the lighter-colored, almost transparent fins.

Serrasalmus notatus; red-bellied piranha: Orinoco, Lago del Guarico, and scattered locales in Venezuela. This species reaches the length of about 10 inches and is very similar to the red-bellied piranha in overall appearance, except for the presence of a large, prominent humeral (shoulder) spot. This fades somewhat in older specimens, but is usually present in all age groups and quite noticeable. The base of the caudal fin has a diffuse, blackish base and the lower lobe is often assymetrically elongated. This is an aggressive and nervous fish that cannot be trusted when under stress or crowded in the aquarium.

Catoprion mento, the wimple piranha: the Lower Amazon, Bolivia, and the

This closeup of the piranha's formidable teeth and jaw structure should serve as a warning to the incautious finger-dipper!

There are two species of *Catoprion*. The fish with the single anal and dorsal fin spine, shown above, is *Catoprion mento*. The fish with the double anal and dorsal first rays, shown below, is called by some Gery's wimple piranha and is considered to be a separate (and as yet undescribed) species.

A closeup of the anal fin of *Catoprion.*

Guianas. Wimple derives from the German *wimpel*, meaning banner. Not classed with the true piranhas, this species is possibly more closely allied to the fishes of the genera *Metynnis* and *Mylosoma*, commonly known as the pacus. The wimple piranha, or Caribe Palometa, has become quite popular in the aquarium hobby over the past few years. It is a small fish, rarely exceeding four inches, and has a nervous rather jittery disposition that makes it advisable to maintain it in a single-species tank if at all possible. Although not a true piranha, the wimple has

general appearance of the real thing, with a strongly underslung lower jaw set with small, though very sharp teeth and an overall humpbacked profile. The dorsal and anal fins are extended into moderate filaments in adult specimens.

The wimple piranha is in part a fin and scale eater in nature and will attack and harass most smaller fishes kept with it. They will usually coexist with larger fishes, though care in the selection of tankmates should be exercised. In personal experience with this species, it was found that when a small prey fish, such as a feeder goldfish, was introduced into a tank containing several adult wimple piranhas, the former was immediately investigated by the wimples and then attacked, tiny bits of fins and a few scales being rapidly clipped from the victim. If the wimples were not overly hungry, they ceased their attacks after a short time and the goldfish was left in peace and not molested again, even when the wimples had developed an appetite once more.

Three photos of *Catoprion*. The young fish is shown in the topmost photo. The double anal is obvious in the bottom fish but the double dorsal spine is not yet developed.

These fish are normally fed smaller feeder fishes, which they will kill if the former are small enough, but the wimple's method of dispatching live fishes can be slow and rather agonizing, so if the hobbyist prefers, live tubifex, bloodworms, and bits of fish or lean beef are eagerly accepted as well. In time, this fish will learn to snatch flake foods from the water's surface.

This species requires soft, slightly acid water and an abundance of plant growth, as it can be a shy creature that appreciates ample hiding places when disturbed. Wimple piranhas exhibit considerable curiosity and will nervously approach and investigate a human hand or finger extended into their tank, but they will rarely, if ever, actually make contact and even if they do, it is a modest nip certainly not worth worrying about!

Three photos showing *Catoprion mento* having varying degrees of elongation of finnage.

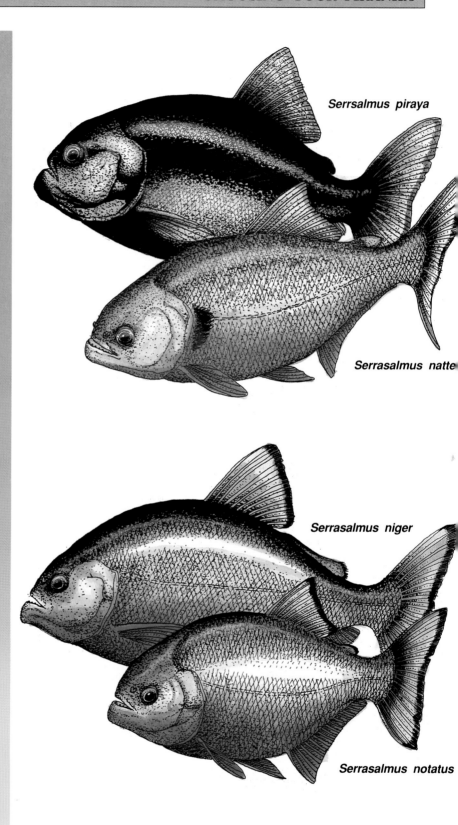

Serrsalmus piraya

Serrasalmus natte

Serrasalmus niger

Serrasalmus notatus

Choosing Your Piranha

The question of which piranha in a tankful is the right one for you boils down essentially to the employment of the two main criteria. When considering any fish species for an aquarium—the health and overall condition of the individual fish, and what other fishes will be kept with it are important. In other words, physical condition and compatibility.

As might be guessed, there are not a whole lot of piranha species available to the hobbyist even today, given the difficulties in collecting and shipping the pugnacious creatures, plus the fact that many, if not most, species are not all that colorful by the usual "tropical fish" standards except when breeding, an act most piranha species seldom carry out in captivity.

By far the commonest piranha species in the aquarium hobby is the attractive red-bellied piranha *(Serrasalmus nattereri).* Several other species, notably the black piranha *(S.*

nigricans), and the so-called gold piranha *(S. aureus)* do occasionally turn up in dealers' tanks, as well as, rarely, one or more of the "pirambebas", such as *S. elongatus,* but all of these are the exception rather than the rule in piranha availability.

The red-bellied piranha, however, enjoys the widest range of piranhas and is the most easily collected in commercial quantity when young, thus the spotted, silvery juveniles are quite often seen in dealers' tanks and no longer considered an oddity today. Young red-bellied piranhas are active and hardy fishes and can serve as a guide for the rest of the group with the exception of the specialized wimple piranhas, which have already been discussed separately.

Nearly all piranhas are active predators and are known to be cannibalistic under some circumstances, so any specimen being considered for purchase should be carefully examined

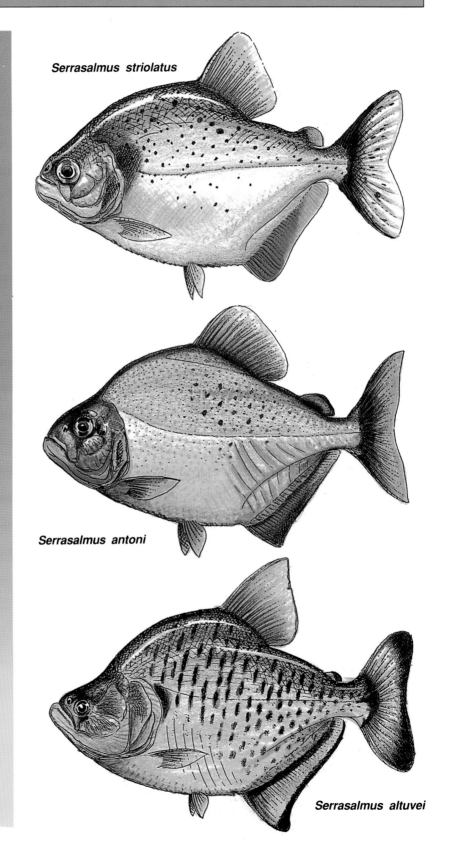

Serrasalmus striolatus

Serrasalmus antoni

Serrasalmus altuvei

for fin and body damage inflicted by a tankmate. Piranhas possess amazing powers of regeneration of lost fins or body flesh, but as with any fish being considered for purchase, it is never wise to select an individual with several strikes against it from the start.

When unnaturally confined and under stress, young piranhas will often attack each others' eyes, simply because these organs are the largest and most visible. One-eyed piranhas are regrettably common in dealers' tanks and are sometimes offered, more as a gag, at half-price.

Most dealers maintain young piranhas in display tanks abundantly decorated with plastic plants in order to "dither," or distract the fish and give them plenty of opportunity to avoid each other; specimens kept under these conditions are much more likely to reach the hobbyist in an undamaged state and in good health.

Other than obvious fin and body damage, the criteria for the selection of a healthy piranha are precisely those observed when purchasing any other aquarium fish: look for an active, alert fish with a robust body, good color, blemish-free finnage, and an absence of any obvious disease or parasitic infestation. If possible, observe the fish being fed and try to select those specimens that feed actively but concentrate on the food offered and not on each other in the excitement. A young piranha that makes repeated passes at (or contact with) its tankmates during normal feeding may well continue that undesirable behavioral trait as it matures, with more ominous results.

Piranhas have the peculiar habit of dashing madly about when disturbed and lodging themselves among the plants or even lying on their sides on the bottom. This bizarre behavior is certainly not reassuring to the new piranha purchaser but it can be considered a normal fright response and not a real drawback if the fish are otherwise healthy and active. Needless to say, care should be taken to minimize the stress to the fish every step of the way in order to avoid this kind of behavior and the scale damage that could well result in the close confines of the aquarium.

Serrasalmus manueli

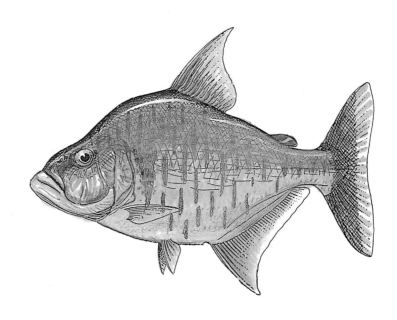

Serrasalmus spilopleura

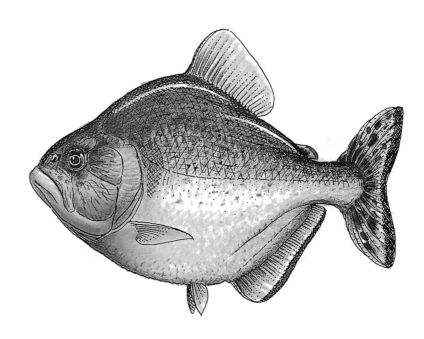

Handling Piranhas

In the course of its contact with man, the freshly-collected piranha will pass through many hands, from those of the initial collector in the Amazon Basin through those of the importer, wholesaler, and· retailer to the hobbyist who finally introduces the by now well-traveled fish to its new home in the living room tank. Not all of those hands will have been encased in the proverbial "kid gloves," so that by the time a wild piranha arrives in a petshop it will be well versed in the experience of being both roughly and gently handled by an animal it would never normally have encountered in its natural habitat.

The subject of physically handling a piranha, pet or otherwise, is the one that inspires the most apprehension on the part of the beginning aquarist, and indeed, the activity must be carried out with care—from both the human and fish's viewpoint. In spite of its legendary ferocity, the piranha is a surprisingly delicate creature. Like the marine bluefish, the piranha is a fine-scaled fish that is easily injured if roughly handled. Even in the course of careful handling, a good number of the fish's tiny scales may be lost, and if these injuries are extensive enough or penetrate the flesh, the fish may be left wide open to infection and parasite.

Ideally, a large piranha should be moved about as little as possible, but if it must be transported, a sturdy plastic bucket or other such container should be used, for its teeth are quite capable of shredding the average aquarium net. Juveniles under two inches can usually be tackled with a standard mesh net, though the move should be carried out with dispatch, both to reduce the possibility that a hole may be chopped in the net and to protect the piranha itself from injury through abrasion, or "net burn."

When imported, larger specimens are always shipped in double or triple bags of heavy-gauge plastic and packed securely in a styrofoam fish box. Most big piranhas are packed singly and medicated with tranquilizer to keep them calm, for an excited, frantic fish can damage all but the sturdiest of container materials.

Adequately fed, adult piranhas housed in a large aquarium will seldom pose a danger to their owner, but there are a few points to remember in order to lend truth to that statement. First, the aquarist wishing to work in the tank and thus place his hands within reach of the fish should make certain that he has no injuries or open sores that might excite the fish. Any moves should be made slowly and with deliberation so as to avoid unduly frightening the piranhas or placing them in a position in which they feel compelled to attack in self defense. The bottom line rule is one of simple common sense—handle or manipulate objects in the tank as little as possible, and then under low light conditions to minimize disturbance to the fish. If extensive work is required, feed the fish before fooling around in their quarters. If your piranhas seem overly jumpy when you wish to engage in any activity within the tank, postpone it until tomorrow. It should be added that small, juvenile piranhas will only rarely show any interest in a human finger, except to avoid it; the exception to this might be found in thoroughly acclimate fish that have come to associate their owner's hand with food and are hungry when the digit appears in their tank! The bite of a one-inch piranha, however, could be handled with a kiss and a band-aid.

Some localities prohibit the importation or possission of a piranha, for fear they will be released in natural waters.

*Serrasalmus
pingke*

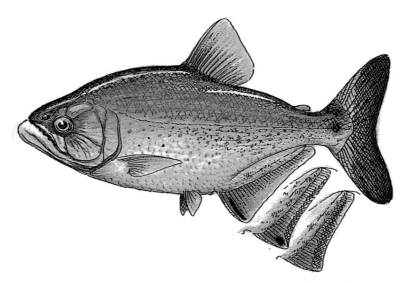

Piranha Quarters

In order to intelligently discuss the question of housing piranhas in the aquarium, it would be advisable to say at least a few words about the fish's natural habitats. We say "habitats," because Neotropical fresh waters can be separated into three general types based on water chemistry and the color of the water itself—blackwater, clearwater, and whitewater.

Black waters, so named because the high degree of organic detritus present on the bottom stains the water a dark tea color, have a low pH (high acidity), low nutrients, poor light penetration, and little in the way of suspended sediments. Most blackwater streams rise in sandy soils of the plains, where dense forests provide a steady and constant supply of fallen leaves. These stain the water so that it may appear almost black from above, but the water itself is quite clear and visibility may be good—up to 3 feet in most areas.

The blackwater streams are often fed by clearwater tributaries. These are almost always shallow, fast-moving watercourses that are also nutrient-poor and have a low pH. These streams often resemble many North American streams in that they have pebbly or rocky substrates and feature scattered deeper pools where fishes may congregate. A number of piranha species are found in these rivers, though in a lower density of biomass (number of individual fishes) than in the next habitat type.

Whitewater rivers are turbid and murky—filled with suspended sediments and very rich in nutrients. This habitat supports the greatest species diversity in fishes as well as the highest biomass—in all native fish species, and piranhas as well. Although many of the more common piranha species, such as the red-bellied piranha, are found in all three habitats, most tend to be more abundant in one type, and this is most often the slower-moving, whitewater rivers. In nature, as a rule, piranhas are restricted to lower altitudes, rarely found

Piranhas must **ALWAYS BE CONSIDERED AS DANGEROUS.** They have teeth, they are predators, and they are animals. Therefore, they must be treated carefully. Imagine if this child was playing in a tank of hungry piranhas instead of peaceful angelfish, *Pterophyllum.*

in mountain streams. It is speculated that the lower prey species density and cooler water inhibit colonization of higher-altitude waters.

Although the hobbyist planning on keeping piranhas may not wish (nor be able) to

close proximity except at feeding time. Thus the hobbyist contemplating keeping them must be prepared to provide them with roomy quarters. This means a tank no smaller than 20 gallons capacity for two to

four small fish, much larger if possible. As with most fishes, and indeed all wild animals in confinement, there is no such thing as too large an enclosure, be it a home aquarium or a zoo habitat. Ample space will enable the piranhas to move freely about without undue contact with each other and under the right conditions, to spawn in captivity.

This is the safest kind of aquarium for piranhas. It's almost impossible to put your hand in accidentally without knowing how to open the top!

duplicate the murky nature of the whitewater environment in the home aquarium, the essentials of the physical habitat can be approximated through the use of peat as a filtering medium and the equipping of the tank with lower wattage lights in order to create the subdued situations most piranha species appear to prefer in the wild state.

All piranhas are highly active fishes, on the move ceaselessly and fairly intolerant of each others'

The ideal situation for, say, six two-inch juvenile piranhas, would be a 55-gallon tank; fish of this size will not remain so for very long under good care and favorable environmental conditions. The more growing room you provide, the healthier and more stress-free the fish will be. As piranhas, even very young ones, can be strongly cannibalistic during periods of excitement, it cannot be stressed enough that more room must be provided these fishes than most other tropicals. Too many small piranhas confined in an undersized tank will quickly reduce themselves to a couple of survivors that manage to

temperature changes. Thus, a reliable heater is a must for the well-equipped piranha tank. For the best all-around results, the water temperature should be set at 78°F and maintained at that level.

Although piranhas in nature

Dr. Axelrod photographed these *Serrasalmus aureus* in a public aquarium.

make it to adulthood!

In its neotropical environment the piranha occurs in water of rather benevolent temperature and composition. Water temperatures range from about 75-84°F year-round and are subject to relatively little fluctuation, so that in captivity, the piranha is fairly intolerant of sharp

prefer soft, slightly acid water (a pH of 6.5 and a hardness of about 10 DH) with an abundance of organic detritus, they are quite adaptable where it comes to water chemistry. The fish has been successfully maintained and even bred at pH values up to 8.5 and a hardness of 18-19 DH. But the ideal aquarium water chemistry will at least

Serrasalmus nattereri

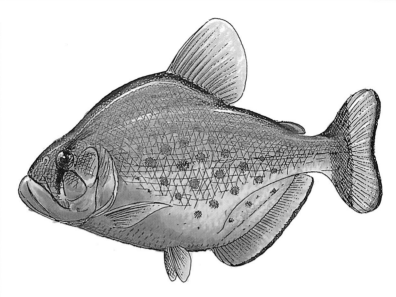

approximate those conditions found in the wild, and this can be accomplished by the use of raw peat fiber or liquid peat extract in the aquarium's filtering system. Your petshop stocks these supplies and can advise you in their correct use. If you can collect natural cedar roots in acid-water "pine barrens" or cedar swamp habitats, these items, after being thoroughly cleaned and boiled, will serve to enhance and maintain soft water conditions in the tank as well.

Catoprion mento

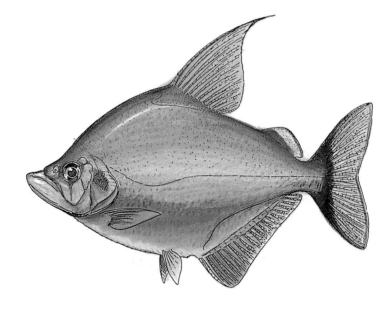

Setting Up the Tank

That piranhas are unusual and very much exotic fishes in every sense of the word there is no doubt, but the preparation of an environment suitable to their needs in captivity is no more off beat than those steps undertaken to set up a tank for a collection of guppies or platies. There is no secret approach to setting up the piranha tank beyond the liberal use of common sense and forethought coupled with attention to initial details that will save the aquarist much grief later on.

The first step in aquarium preparation is to make absolutely certain that the basic hardware item—the tank itself—is spotlessly clean before the substrate and accessories are introduced. This rule should be followed regardless whether the tank was given to you by a friend or purchased spanking-new at a reputable petshop. There are just too many opportunities for bacteria, parasites, or toxic substances to gain entry into an aquarium under the best of conditions, so why take chances with a tank of unknown history or cleanliness?

Many experienced aquarists use a strong Epson salt or artificial seasalt mix solution to clean and disinfect the tank, a method that is both simple and inexpensive. First, place that tank on the firm, level surface it will occupy permanently, fill it with water to within about two inches of the rim and allow about an hour to check for any possible leakage. Better any leaks (which are extremely rare in today's high-quality, all-glass aquaria) are spotted before, rather than after, the aquarium is fully set up and housing piranhas!

Next, the tank should be bailed out so that about two inches of water remains in the bottom. In a 55-gallon aquarium, stir in about two cups of Epson or marinemix salt and allow it to dissolve thoroughly. With a small washcloth, wash all the inner surfaces of the tank thoroughly and repeatedly and then refill the tank with fresh water (and the salt solution) and allow it to stand overnight for complete disinfection. The following day the tank may be emptied and rinsed well with freshwater, dried, and wiped clean of any salt residue, which if present in enough quantity, could prove harmful to the softwater-loving piranhas.

The next step in our "patience is a virtue" procedure is the selection and preparation of the substrate that will serve both as an attraction in the aquarium and the vital growth base for living plants or the anchoring medium for the plastic varieties, if you so choose.

The selection of a suitable substrate involves no small degree of common sense and the resistance of some formidable temptations. Larger pebbles, rocks, shells, marbles, or very coarse gravels are really not wise additions to the piranha tank, attractive though they may be, as they both might contain some soluble salts that may cause trouble later on and they may also provide numerous crevices and crannies into which errant food items that escape the fish's attention may drop and decompose at leisure. A wise rule of thumb to follow when selecting a substrate or planning the

decor of ANY tank is not to arrange any decor items so that either fishes or scavengers are unable to gain access and reach food items which have escaped the notice of the piranhas and drifted out of sight there. Larger rocks of quartz, granite, or plastic are acceptable decor items as they are inert and will not leach salts or other substances into the water, and, if carefully arranged, will lend a natural aspect to the tank.

Medium coarse, natural or white aquarium gravel is the way to go in the choice of basic substrate. Fine beach sand should be avoided as it tends to pack tightly after settling and both prevents plants from rooting satisfactorily and often blackens and turns foul due to lack of adequate water circulation throughout the grains.

As with the tank, the gravel should be washed and rinsed thoroughly before introduction into the tank. In the case of store-bought gravels, repeated washing and rinsing until the water runs clear and free of dust and debris is usually adequate, although allowing the cleaned gravel to stand overnight in a mild salt solution is advisable if its source or cleanliness is at all suspect.

Recommendations as to proper gravel depth vary, but in general, live plants require at the very least an inch of substrate in order to root satisfactorily. The time-honored approach of sloping the gravel from the back to the front of the tank has been pooh-poohed in some circles in recent years, but in general, it's good advice. A gravel depth of three inches at the rear of the tank, sloping to the minimum one-inch at the front, will allow for enough of a rooting bed for larger plants at the rear and, in spite of denials, does indeed encourage debris and waste material to slowly gravitate to the front of the aquarium through the gentle action of the filter flow, where it may be more easily siphoned out.

The piranha tank should contain plants—either live or plastic—and in some abundance, for both the physical and psychological well-being of these shy, often nervous fishes. Some species are strongly vegetarian and will graze on living plants if

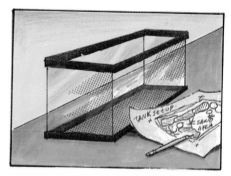

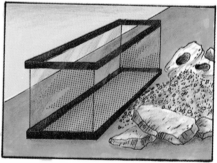

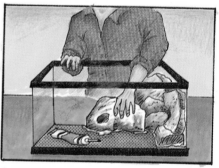

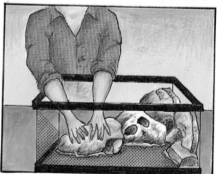

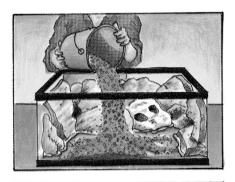

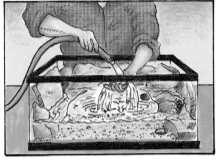

underfed, but in general, all piranhas benefit in a number of ways from a healthy plant growth. As with the average tropical community setup, the aquascaping of piranha quarters should follow the sensible design concept of taller plantings to the rear and sides, shorter toward the front, with the center of the tank left free for unobstructed swimming on the part of the fish, and viewing by the aquarist and interested visitors. Ideally, three-quarters of the tank shoud consist of open space. Bogwood collected in nature and commercially available driftwood pieces can be added as decor items and will provide additional cover and territory for the fish. Be sure to thoroughly clean and boil all such natural decor items before placing them in the tank in order to destroy any potential parasites and remove toxic substances.

Most of the commonly available aquarium plants will serve for the piranha tank, with those of the

5. After washing the sand carefully, add to the tank.

6. Add warm water very slowly, allowing it to flow into your hand so it does not disturb the sand.

7. Leaving a few inches of room for the water to expand, adjust all the other decorations such as ornaments and plants.

8. Add a bit more water but do not fill to the top. Put on the hood and lights and allow the water to age for a few days.

Hamilton's deluxe lighting system for all kinds of aquariums. Hamilton also makes a light enhancing, electro-white reflector.

Energy Savers makes a whole range of lighting devices with different kinds of housings and lamps.

Your local petshop should be able to show you suitable lights for your piranha aquarium.

Energy Savers makes high output lamp hood.

genera *Sagittaria, Vallisneria, Cryptocoryne,* and *Aponogeton* being particularly well suited to the purpose. Fine-leaved plants, such as *Cabomba* and *Myriophyllum,* should be included as nest-building material if the eventual object is spawning the fish. If light conditions permit, the various small floating plants such as *Lemna* and *Salvinia* can be added; these will serve as a light-diffusing surface cover and a significant food item for some piranha species.

The question of light and how much of it can be an important one for the piranha hobbyist. Given the fishes' shy and somewhat nervous disposition, not to mention the nature of the natural habitat, piranhas in the wild generally frequent tree-shaded, rainforest watercourses that feature lower light conditions. When possible, captive conditions should duplicate that environment as closely as

possible for optimum health. The use of warm white fluorescent tubes will achieve a softer, less intimidating light level and yet provide more than adequate viewing of the fish.

Once the tank has been set up and permitted to age for about three days, the newly-purchased piranhas can be introduced, but here again, care is required. As with most warmwater tropical aquarium fishes, most piranhas are transported from petshop to home packed in small plastic bags, these usually doubled up to prevent the fish from puncturing the plastic with their already impressive teeth. As with other tropicals, piranhas should be "floated" in their bag for at least 20 minutes before release into their new home so that the respective temperatures are at the same level. Having gone through the repeated ordeal of handling and alien surroundings in their long, stressful journey from the natural environment to the tank of the hobbyist, the new arrivals will be understandably jittery. For this reason, it is best to release the piranhas into their quarters slowly and with as much

tender loving care as possible. This is best accomplished in the evening, with the tank's lights out and under lower ambient light conditions in the room. Resist the temptation to simply upend the bag and let the fish go; instead, gradually

The gravel you use on the bottom can be natural or colored. The tank should be organized before any water is added. The model is setting plastic plants in place.

Artificial shale rocks and caves are available from your local petshop. Aeration is a necessity for almost all aquariums.

position the bag sideways and allow the fish to swim out in their own good time. Piranhas unceremoniously dumped into a tank for the first time usually dart frantically about, lodging themselves among the plants or even injuring themselves against the gravel substrate. With a little patience (again, always a virtue in the aquarium hobby!) this unnecessary trauma can be avoided.

Once introduced and in a state of relative calm, young piranhas will usually form a loose yet closely integrated group, each individual oriented into the filter's current flow and poised in a slight downward angle, as though ready for instant flight. As long as their unease with their new surroundings persists, they will find comfort in the close proximity of their own kind and maintain it, much as most smaller fishes find safety in a dense school configuration when confronted with a predator in the wild.

Within a few hours, though, they will begin to stake out territories in the tank and actively threaten each other and even attack inanimate or floating objects. It is at this time that the attention paid prior to aquascaping the tank proves valuable, for under acclimated, established conditions, the piranhas will station themselves on or near their home territories, schooling up only when disturbed or feeding.

Given the jittery nature of piranhas in general, a tank which provides the maximum in the way of "privacy" would be in the hobbyist's and the fish's best interest, especially if one has any hope or intention of breeding the fish. The ideal setup in this respect would be one in which the front of the tank is the sole viewing surface, the other three panels being either of wood or fiberglass construction, or the aquarium set into a wall unit. A conventional aquarium "photo background" will serve to mask off the rear of a tank placed in an open room situation, and additional sections of background can be secured to the sides in order to give the fishes the greatest possible sense of security. Piranhas maintained in a

Large displays of plastic plants enable you to furnish an aquarium to suit your individual taste.

totally exposed tank, with
much human activity
swirling all about them,
will not be contented fish
and will likely never
develop the degree of ease
required to even entertain
the notion of spawning.

Although piranhas are
remarkably adaptable and
resilient fishes that can
endure a considerable
amount of abuse before
succumbing, they are
tropical fishes that
originate in an environment
that experienced very little
in the way of temperature
fluctuations throughout the
course of the year. For this

Above:
*Catoprion
mento* in a
densely
planted
aquarium.
Below:
Attaching the
heater/
thermostat
combination
unit to the rim
of the
aquarium.

A glass-cleaner is a MUST for the piranha tank. You shouldn't stick your hand into the tank to clean the glass. Use the glass-cleaner wand. The notched end is for prodding plants into position.

The Whisper 200 is a vibrator airpump suitable for a small tank. There are many sizes of airpumps available through your local petshop.

The Fluval canister pump is both pump and filter. Canister filters do a great job in polishing water.

reason, a reliable aquarium heater is a must in the piranha tank, and the additional use of a good-quality, snug-fitting tank hood is more than a good idea. A good tank light hood and cover will not only help eliminate drafts that will adversely affect the temperature of the aquarium, it will control your piranha's inclination to travel in an upward and outward direction. An untoward trip to the carpet must be avoided at all costs, as piranhas, much more so than most other fishes, are in reality quite delicate and cannot readily withstand the tremendous stress and trauma resulting from even a few minutes of

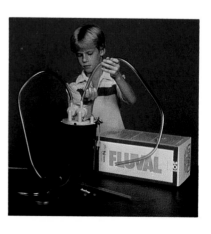

flopping about on a dry surface loaded with landborne bacteria. So—keep that piranha tank well covered!

It can be summed up that that as much room as possible should be provided; plenty of physical opportunities for territory setup made available to them; and considerable care taken to avoidance of

the environmental requirements of piranhas kept in confinement differ little from those common sense conditions provided nearly all other fishes, coldwater or tropical, with the exception temperature fluctuations. Given reasonable attention to these few inflexible physical parameters, the average aquarist should experience few trials and travails in the adventure of piranha care and culture.

A cross-section of an ideal piranha aquarium. The undergravel filter is terraced to hold back the sand and to maximize filtration.

Petshops have many different types of water test kits for testing pH and other chemical characteristics.

Diatomite canister filters are excellent for water polishing.

The Question of Feeding

Piranhas are typical of the cruising and ambush predators among fishes in that when hungry (which is most of the time) they will make swift, investigative feeding passes at virtually any small object of interest they encounter in their environment. For this reason it is always somewhat risky to attempt to maintain any piranha species in a community tank situation. In captivity, piranhas are usually offered larger living foods, such as feeder goldfish or guppies, for these animals most closely approximate the natural prey and always trigger the feeding response in healthy piranhas. But the captive diet need not nor should not be restricted to this fare alone. Many piranha owners offer their charges live feeder fishes only for the obvious reason—watching such a superbly-adapted predator stalk, strike, and dispatch its prey is an exciting experience, no doubt about it. Feeder fishes

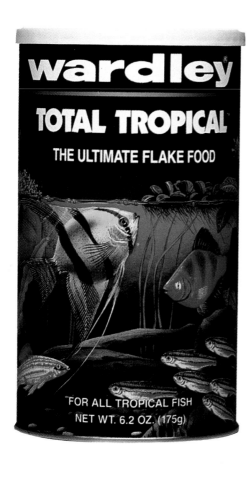

Piranhas can easily be trained to accept normal tropical fish food.

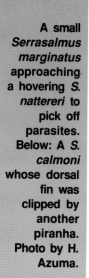

A small *Serrasalmus marginatus* approaching a hovering *S. nattereri* to pick off parasites. Below: A *S. calmoni* whose dorsal fin was clipped by another piranha. Photo by H. Azuma.

are indeed essential to the piranha diet as they provide the required calcium and other minerals that are usually not made available through conventional fishfoods or even invertebrate prey. But as noted before, the spectacle of the piranha's efficiency as a killer is, or should be, only a part of the fish's appeal as a living creature and should certainly not be the sole motivation for keeping them.

Ichthyologists Leo G. Nico and Donald C. Taphorn conducted extensive studies on the diet of wild piranhas, analyzing the stomach contents of over 1000 wild-collected individual specimens of seven species. Their findings demonstrated that the more elongate, sharp-nosed species specialize on the fins and scales of the prey fishes, while the blunt-headed, heavy jawed species (such as the red-bellied piranha) prefer the fish flesh, usually taking the entire target fish, or at least a good amount of it, in an attack. Species between the two extremes in body shape show a combination of the two diets, showing that overall piranha morphology (body shape) has evolved with the object of diet specialization in mind.

Food and feeding habits also vary among the different piranha size classes as well as from season to season, even within a single species. In the red-bellied piranha, for example, the very young, free-swimming fry (0.6 inches or under) feed almost exclusively on copepods and other tiny crustacean organisms, switching primarily to aquatic insects as they grow larger. By the time they are about three inches long, the young fish are almost entirely piscivorous, attacking other small fishes

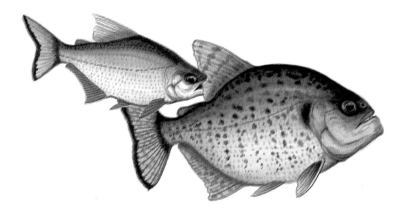

Serrasalmus marginatus clipping off a piece of dorsal from an *S. spilopleura.*

close to their own size.

In the case of the scale-eating pike piranha *(S. elongatus),* the diet is much more specialized throughout the growth cycle. Although very small individuals also consume tiny crustaceans, those individuals larger than one inch in standard length restrict themselves almost entirely to the finnage of other small fishes, very often those with which the juvenile piranhas actively albeit surreptitiously school. Adult *S. elongatus* take the fins and scales of larger fishes, as well as pieces of flesh or smaller, whole fishes.

Based on direct observation in the wild, the fascinating feeding behavior of the pikepiranha involves a sort of predatory mimicry and has been studied in both the aquarium and in the wild. The fish's general strategy is to unobtrusively place itself

among prey fishes of similar appearance (such as larger, silvery tetras) and maneuver until it can make a strike. It then attacks swiftly, grabs an unpaired fin with its long jaws, and, using its own body for leverage and torque, twists violently until it comes away with a manageable piece of fin. In the wild, the pike piranha has been observed to consistently travel with schools of large tetras, skillfully and quickly taking repeated bites from the fins of its victims without alarming the rest of the school. Truly, an aquatic wolf in sheep's clothing.

It has been noted that fin-eating piranhas are one of the main reasons why ichthyologists have come to use the Standard Length measurement (the length of the fish from the snout to the base of the caudal fin) as opposed to Total Length (the

Most quality petshops have a wide range of aquarium fish foods. Your piranhas can be trained to eat almost all fish foods, especially pellets. You should feed ALL aquarium fishes as varied a diet as possible. Don't rely on a single brand or a single kind. Always alternate flakes and pellets.

Quinn 1990

length from the snout to the end of the caudal fin) when measuring Neotropical fishes. Even the larger, more aggressive whole-fish-eating piranhas are preyed upon in this manner by the fin and scale eaters and thus the caudal fins of the former are often only partly regenerated, making an accurate measurement difficult.

Those piranhas that consume mostly fish flesh or the entire prey animal generally grow at a faster rate than the members of the fin and scale-eating group. For example, the red-bellied piranha reaches the standard length of between five and eight inches by its second rainy season whereas the pike piranha subsisting on the less nutritious diet of fins or scales, seldom exceeds six inches standard length at the age of one year. However, the fin-eaters usually reach sexual maturity at a much smaller size and the breeding population thus consists of smaller individuals on average.

In nature, and in the aquarium as well, most of the larger, fish-eating species

Serrasalmus rhombeus about to make a meal of a freshwater shrimp.

adopt a "hang in there and wait" strategy of food procurement, although many potential prey animals are located and recognized as such through vibrations sent through the water when they are injured or entangled in nets and acting accordingly. Most of the larger piranha species are, in fact, by nature ambush predators that make full use of rock and root cover in the substrate or streamside to lie in wait and pick off unsuspecting prey. Groups of red-bellied piranhas ranging in number from five to more than 100 individuals will also wait in ambush at favorable locations along the stream banks; brushy windfalls, deeper pools, the bases of small waterfalls, and sharp angles in the watercourse's flow often attract both cruising schools of piranhas and solitary individuals

seeking unwary or distressed smaller fishes.

Although piranhas are certainly skilled hunters, unless a target fish is unhealthy or in some way distressed, most would-be victims are alert enough to successfully avoid predation by piranhas. The fin and scale eaters are those piranha species most able to actually chase down and grab a healthy fish in open water but the majority of species depend on the swift investigatory pass and give up the chase if the intended victim is able to easily outdistance its pursuer. This hunting strategy can be observed as well in such terrestrial predators as the wild dog and cheetah of Africa, both of which will effect brief sorties in the direction of a prey animal, and continue the pursuit only if the target animal appears

Serrasalmus nattereri making a meal of a small tetra after a short chase.

confused or can be approached closely enough so that a successful kill can be reasonably anticipated.

Fishes by far comprise the bulk of the diet of wild piranhas, but other vertebrates are often taken as food when the opportunity presents itself. Analyses of the stomach contents of the Orinoco red-bellied piranha have turned up bird fragments, the flesh and skin of snakes and small caimans, and the fur and flesh of small mammals. In the case of the presence of bird fragments, piranhas are known to congregate in some numbers in the water beneath heron and egret rookeries, immediately attacking any nestling that happens to fall from the safety of the nest. Researchers working with piranhas in the wild always caution against blissful wading or engaging in other aquatic activity in the immediate vicinity of bird rookeries for these locations will almost always harbor

active and hungry crowds of piranhas that have learned that food is to be had there.

Captive piranhas are seldom offered such varied and exotic fare, but they will accept a wide variety of living and prepared foods, from tubificid and bloodworms through earthworms and cut lean beef and fish to flakes and pellets. Juveniles under two inches will also eagerly accept live brine shrimp, mosquito larvae, and glassworms.

As might be expected, it is at feeding time that the piranha's vaunted ferocity and agility comes to the fore, and, consequently, when the risk of injury in the confines of an aquarium are at their highest, particularly if the tank is of inadequate size. When food items, be they live or dead, are introduced into the tank, every fish at once becomes keenly alert and aware of its presence. Little actual, deliberate stalking of the prey is carried out—the fish simply

This _Geophagus_ has learned to dart into the face of the piranha to make it flee. In general fishes with their fins flared are the aggressors, while fishes with their fins clamped or partially closed are the victims.

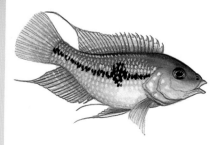

effect short, nervous forays in its direction and then the actual feeding is instituted by one or more individuals that attack in swift dashes, snapping up small prey items whole and chopping neat pieces from larger food items with a "shivering" action that spans mere seconds. The instant involvement of every piranha in the tank in the feeding action is quite reminiscent of and similar to the famous "feeding frenzy" behavior observed in sharks; though each fish clearly knows the difference between its conspecifics and the food

at hand, mistakes do occur in the ensuing mayhem and some scale and fin damage may be the result. All the more reason to provide the fish with more than enough room to maneuver about in and find shelter after feeding.

Following active feeding, piranhas will normally retreat to their respective territories and enter a period of passivity during which the food is digested. At this time they will normally orient themselves into the water current flow in order to receive the increased oxygen required for more effective

Piranhas do not eat snails because they lack the crushing molar-type teeth necessary to crush the shells. These common aquarium snails are useful in the piranha aquarium.

It may sound cruel, but it is nature's way. Goldfish which indicate they are dying by hanging listlessly in the water may be fed to piranhas which dispatch them very quickly...usually biting them in half with their first attack.

digestion.

Under most circumstances, captive piranhas should be fed modest portions of hearty live or cut foods every day or larger portions every other day. As with all aquarium fishes, they should be offered only what they can clean up completely in five or so minutes. Contrary to popular belief, scavengers can be included in the tank and may clear away leftovers; these will be discussed later. Adult piranhas quite often enter periods of abstinence during which they will refuse all foods offered, up to and including feeder fishes; this behavior is part of the normal cycle and under most conditions ends within two or three days.

As with most other larger, carnivorous aquarium fishes, piranhas can be rather messy eaters, due to the nature of the food, leaving some suspended debris and resultant clouding in the water. For this reason, the use of a canister filter is advised, with auxiliary filtration provided by an outside power filter if possible. The filter elements should be cleaned or replaced more often (about once a week is fine) than is the case in the conventional community tank.

A comparison of a piranha and a pacu. Though their coloration is the same, their mouth parts and gill covers are different.

A head-on view of three piranhas. A., *S. marginatus* is hardly a danger to anything because of its weak jaw and body. The middle fish is B., *S. spilopleura*, a piranha which can be considered a danger, while C., *S. nattereri* is the true piranha type.

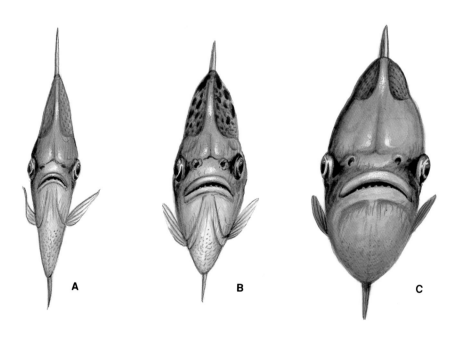

A   B   C

Suitable Tankmates

It is a common belief among the great majority of hobbyists that piranhas are suited only to the single-species tank or that they can only be maintained in "solitary confinement"—that is, a single fish all by its lonesome. In fact, these fishes can and do coexist with an amazing variety of other species, even those normally considered their natural prey!

To begin a discussion of piranha tankmates it need only be stated that these fishes coexist with many other fish families and species in the natural community, the essential key to mutual survival there being the matter of adequate (indeed, unlimited) space in which the normal predator/prey escape and avoidance relationship can function. In the unnatural confines of the aquarium, that relationship cannot, of course, exist as freely and uninhibited as it would in nature and thus the issue of suitable cohabitants must be approached with much more caution and forethought.

Piranhas react both to the action of the prey and to some degree its color; it has been demonstrated that the color red appears to trigger the attack response in some piranhas, thus bright red feeder goldfish are assaulted at once while the more drab, wild forms of goldfish or carp are often ignored. This guide can be employed in the matter of tankmates as well. As is often the case with many larger, highly predatory fishes, catfishes and other bottom-dwelling scavengers of drab brown or grayish coloration and cryptic pattern make the best and most logical tankmates. Algae-eaters of the catfish genera *Hypostomus* or *Ancistrus* are the best choices here as they are large enough to avoid arousing the culinary interest of the piranhas kept with them and armored enough to survive a nip or two if they do come to a piranha's attention. Smaller and more active and colored catfishes such as members of the *Corydoras* and *Synodontis* genera would be at slightly higher risk in a piranha tank, though if the latter are adequately fed, the danger will be minimized considerably. Remember that any sudden, erratic, or disoriented behavior on the part of a piranha tankmate may well trigger the attack response; it is wise to judge any suitable tankmates on the basis of their normal behavior as well. "Keeping a low profile" would seem to be the key to getting along in a piranha tank!

A number of the other "conventional" scavengers popular in the aquarium hobby can be safely housed in the tank containing adult piranhas as long as their selection is made with some forethought. The so-called Chinese algae-eater *(Gyrinocheilus aymonieri)* has

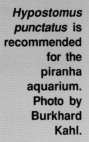

Hypostomus punctatus is recommended for the piranha aquarium. Photo by Burkhard Kahl.

Ancistrus chagresi can be kept with piranhas. Photo by D. Conkel. These fish (as well as the *Hypostomus*) are found in nature along with piranhas.

been successfully kept with piranhas, particularly when both are of smaller size; as these fish grow, they become more active and somewhat aggressive and thus may attract the attentions of their piranha tankmates in a most unwanted way!

Most snail species are a safe bet in a piranha tank as neither their color (generally somber) nor their activity (slow-motion) act as attack triggers. Snails are diligent scavengers that will devour algae and most organic waste and they have the added "benefit" of the ability to reproduce themselves, sometimes to a prodigious degree, without the help of the aquarist. The more popular types are the large apple, or livebearing snails, the attractive red ramshorn, and the various species of small pond snails. Among the latter are those species likely to become a real problem due to overpopulation of a tank and they can be a real challenge to eradicate. Keep in mind that in addition to a fondness for algae, which aquarists tend to discourage in their tanks, snails may well wreak considerable havoc on live aquarium plants.

Although piranhas have been successfully maintained, albeit somewhat gingerly, with guppies, cichlids, and characins, the risk of accident is obviously very much higher and really not worth taking. An exception to the rule are the large characins of the genus *Metynnis,* commonly known as "silver dollars." One species, *M. roosevelti* closely resembles the red-bellied piranha in both form and color pattern—a striking example of protective mimicry, as both species coexist well enough in the wild state. The silver dollar is

Synodontis alberti, from Africa, can also be kept with South America's piranhas. Photo by Burkhard Kahl.

This young *Metynnis mola* looks so much like a young piranha due to its coloration and spot pattern, but the small mouth and weak jaws give it away. Actually *Metynnis* are vegetarians. Photo by Dr. Herbert R. Axelrod.

Asia's *Gyrinocheilus aymonieri* can also be kept with piranhas. Photo by Burkhard Kahl.

Armored catfishes from South America, like this *Hoplosternum pectorale*, can be kept with piranhas. Photo by Burkhard Kahl.

dollar is a predominantly vegetarian fish that occurs in the same habitats and often schools with piranhas in the wild. The species had a red blush on the abdominal region that closely approximates that of *S. nattereri* and thus renders it immune to attack under most circumstances. In the aquarium, *M. roosevelti* can be safely housed with the red-bellied piranha as long as the respective individuals are of the same size.

Adult piranhas of nearly all species can also be maintained in aquaria under "school" conditions—again, as long as all of the individuals are of approximately the same size. But care must be exercised, for few aspects of the behavior of virtually any animal, let alone piranhas, are entirely predictable and accidents can happen. At times, particularly during feeding activity, conflicts may arise and violent contact made between individuals, but under most circumstances the damage inflicted is not extensive and the piranha's considerable regenerative powers usually effect a healing within a few days. The rule of thumb, however, should be that any fish observed to be sustaining body or fin damage on a regular basis should be isolated from the rest until a complete healing of injuries takes place.

The cardinal rule here is that under no circumstances should any attempt be made to mix the various scale or fin-eating species with those piranhas that feed on whole fishes; in nature, the fin eaters regularly attack even the larger piranha species, snatching bits of fin or scale with impunity. This behavior will almost certainly be carried over into the aquarium environment, with obvious consequences.

It should go without saying that the less disturbance captive piranhas are subjected to, the better for all concerned. Any community setup containing piranhas is at best an uneasy alliance, and a sudden move on the part of the hobbyist or undue fooling around in the tank could trigger a defensive attack response or simply change the "balance of power" to the degree that a tankmate formerly unmolested is summarily dispatched. One need not approach the piranha tank with abject paranoia— just tread with caution and don't tap on it to show your fishes off to visitors!

This is a rare *Metynnis*. It is barred, as you can see, but it is also covered with parasites. These parasites eventually hatch out and die harmlessly in the aquarium. Photo by Aaron Norman.

Keeping Your Piranha Healthy

Maintaining your piranhas in a state of continual good health involves exactly those procedures and precautions observed and carried out for any other living animal, up to and including yourself: careful attention to diet, the elimination of stress, and providing a clean, disease-free environment.

A number of factors account for the unnecessary loss of fishes in captivity. Chief among them are:

• OVERCROWDING: This is the one single factor that is usually at the root of most unexplained aquarium fish deaths. Even the most mysterious cases of fish mortality ("everything in my tank seemed to be fine") can be, if probed deeply enough, traced back to the fact that simply too many fishes were being kept in the tank so that they exceeded its limited carrying capacity. If fishes are crowded, they will be subject to much more stress and a much greater amount of carbon dioxide than is desirable will be present in the water. Infectious diseases will also spread like wildfire in a smaller tank jammed with too many fishes.

• TEMPERATURE: In all tropical aquaria, drastic temperature fluctuations (either up or down) should be avoided at all costs. Though many fish species have a wide tolerance of erratic temperatures, piranhas are not among them, unless the change is effected very gradually. In addition, overly high temperatures may serve to activate certain parasites, while lower temperatures trigger activation in others.

• LIGHT: Although most tropical fishes are quite tolerant of great variation in the quality and the duration of artificial lighting, it is generally agreed among experienced aquarists that the direction of the light is of greater importance. Side-lighting produces stress in most fishes, while that coming from above—the natural direction—obviously duplicates natural conditions and thus is by far the best.

A school of young piranhas. They are overcrowded and will start biting each other.

• WATER CHEMISTRY: The proper level of acidity or alkalinity (known as the level of pH) varies according to the types of fishes, but in general, marine fishes usually require a pH of about 8.0, or slightly alkaline, while freshwater fishes do best at a pH level of 7.0, or neutral. Exceptions to this rule are those fishes occuring in estuarine situations, where the pH may vary widely, according to the tidal flow or the distance from the sea.

• AERATION AND WATER FLOW: Some gases found in water, such as carbon dioxide, nitrogen, and hydrogen sulphide, are harmful to fishes if present in excess and these can be removed or dissipated by efficient filtration and water action.

• WASTE PRODUCTS: Organic waste from the decay of plants or the normal bodily functions of fishes will not harm most fishes unless it builds to a level which produces ammonia and nitrites in concentration, at which time it becomes toxic.

• DIET: As with people, a diet lacking in variety, and consequently in vitamins and other nutritional essentials, will cause deficiencies in

Harald Schultz photographed this *Metynnis* that was caught in a school of piranhas. The red belly marking is normal but it looks like a wound.

This *Metynnis luna* was bitten by a piranha while both were being netted. Photo by Hans-Joachim Richter.

fishes that leave them open to stress, disease, and parasitic infestation. It is wise to avoid reliance on prepared foods alone, but rather to vary this diet with live and frozen foods whenever possible.

And remember that whatever the nature of the foods offered, observe that cardinal aquarium law— DON'T OVERFEED!

• HANDLING: Needless to say, once a fish has been introduced into its new home, it should be moved or handled as little as possible, if at all. Even careful handling, carried out with patience and the right equipment, may result in seemingly minor scale or fin damage that serve as sites for attack by harmful disease organisms.

• PARASITES: Many kinds of organisms parasitize fishes, some of them quite specific, others much more general and

The top fish is a female *Serrasalmus gibbus*, while the lower fish is a male. Photos by Hiroshi Azuma.

thus a threat to an entire community of fishes. Many medications are available on the market today, and while most of them are quite effective when used as directed against specific diseases and parasites, there is no such thing as a "cure-all" for fishes. One of the most venerable, and in many ways, proven medications used over the years for the effective treatment of "Ich" and other more contagious fish diseases is the salt bath. Salt can be introduced as a mild solution to an entire tank in the proportion of about one teaspoonful per gallon of water, or it, employed as a stronger bath agent (3 tablespoons of salt per gallon) in which the afflicted fish is "dipped" for a period of between one and three minutes.

In the end, there's no

Serrasalmus calmoni. The edges of the tail were chewed off and regenerated...but the new area was not pigmented.

substitute for the old axiom: "an ounce of prevention is worth a pound of cure." Veteran aquarists usually adhere to the following rules in an effort to head off problems before they occur:

• Never add a newly-acquired fish to an established aquarium until it has been observed in quarantine for a few days.

New fishes should ideally be given a brief salt treatment to eliminate any possible resident parasites.

• Sick fishes should be provided separate quarters and placed there at the first sign of trouble.

• When sick fishes consistently turn up in a community aquarium, the tank should be put through

a thorough process of cleaning and sterilization for the spores of contagious diseases may be very persistent and remain dormant and survive even strong medication.

• After parasitization, overcrowding and overfeeding are the second and third most common causes of disease in fishes.

Avoid these pitfalls!

• Chlorine added to drinking water may be beneficial to its human recipients but it is harmful to fishes; use a dechlorinating compound or allow water to stand at least 24 hours to permit the gas to dissipate before using it in an aquarium!

This Amazonian pirambeb is *Serrasalmus serrulatus* collected and photographed by Dr. Herbert R. Axelrod. This was a wildcaught fish on a hook-and-line, yet it had a few chunks taken out of its tail during the brief period it dangled helplessly

This is a tank-raised hybrid piranha. Probably a cross between *S. nattereri* and *S. gibbus* or *S. aureus.* Photo by Dr. Herbert R. Axelrod.

Captive Breeding

The reproduction and growth of piranhas in the natural state is still poorly understood and most of the data comes from collections made over a period of a year or more. As with most fish species in the tropics, piranha reproduction is closely tied to the wet and dry seasonal cycle. Young red-bellied piranhas of about five inches in length appear to mature sexually just before the start of the rainy season. With the onset of the rains, usually in April, spawning commences and continues through July. Some species may spawn again in late summer if conditions are favorable.

During the breeding season, many piranha species undergo an often striking color change. The red-bellied species, for example, is a steely blue and silvery with a bright red belly for most of the year, but with the onset of the spawning period, sexually mature adults of both sexes become a deep black, adorned with myriad flecks of glittering gold and purple. The fins, normally transparent with black edges, also become very dark. Like the trout's, the piranha's body color at this time is photochromatic—that is, it is highly sensitive to light, so much that if a piece of paper or cloth is placed over the body of a dark, breeding piranha, the covered area will wash out and fade almost instantly.

For the most part, piranhas are substrate spawners that build something of a nest among vegetation and bottom detritus and deposit the adhesive eggs in a relatively compact mass that is zealously guarded by both parents or by the male alone.

The spawning of any piranha species in captivity must be regarded as a rare and exceptional event; conditions must be just right and the potential breeders ready and fully compatible with each other. The majority of captive spawnings have occurred—pretty much spontaneously—in the large tanks of public aquariums, several in Europe. The first documented captive spawning was apparently that of *Serrasalmus spilopleura* in Chicago's John G. Shedd Aquarium in 1960. In that

SPAWNING
OF
SERRASALMUS
GIBBUS BY
HIROSHI
AZUMA

The male
starts chasing
the female
trying to drive
her into the
nest.

A clump of
eggs is laid.
The white
ones are
infertile.

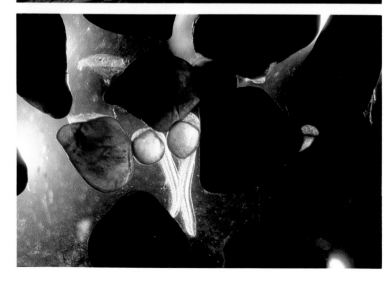

The young
quickly
develop.

Still attached to the egg case, this fry is about to emerge.

The fry escapes the egg case and becomes free-swimming.

In a month it already looks like a piranha.

case, the fish had been maintained in a 1200 gallon tank for about three years and were seven inches long. The eggs were deposited on water plants and the spawn and the resultant fry were guarded by the male.

A number of private individuals have managed the accomplishment as well, and one of these successful spawnings will be discussed below.

The red-bellied piranha becomes quite active and much more aggressive when ready to spawn. The fish show signs of nest building activity, destroying or removing plants in the vicinity and moving about other small objects in the tank in the preparation of a shallow depression to receive the eggs, much as cichlids and temperate sunfishes are prone to do. There is no set rule for

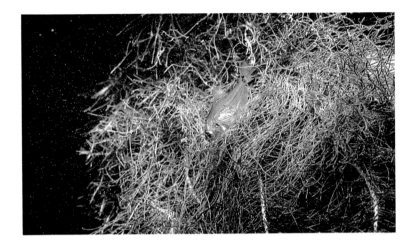

During the spawning of *Serrasalmus spilopleura*, this youngster swims by the spawning nest. Photo by I. Sazima.

determining breeding readiness, but Schulte writes that the red-bellied piranha undergoes color changes that are characteristic of the onset of spawning: *"Overall, the animals grow lighter in color, the red color in the abdominal region becomes more intense, and the general iridescence greatly diminishes."* These factors, coupled with the fish's growing restlessness and aggression toward all

These plants were cut during the pre-spawning ritual of *Serrasalmus gibbus.* Photo by H. Azuma.

other fishes, should indicate that a spawning attempt is imminent.

The principal requirement for spawning piranhas in the aquarium is that of tank size; any serious attempt to breed them should not be made in a tank of less than 200 gallons capacity, preferably larger. The reasons for this are manifold: given the piranha's generally aggressive and territorial nature at all times, the onset of spawning heightens this behavior to the point that conflicts are almost inevitable and may be fatal if the adult fish are too tightly confined.

European aquarists have had the best luck with small groups of between six and 10 individuals that have been determined to be ripe and ready to spawn. As there is little or no sexual dimorphism among piranhas and no external sex differences are apparent, the technique used with angelfish of raising the prospective breeders from fry and allowing them to pair off naturally serves best with piranhas as well. When dealing with only a hoped-for pair of the fish, the usual practice is to place the ripe female in the tank a day or two prior to the introduction of the male. If the fish are compatible and ready to spawn, the male will quickly darken to a violet-black color so that his iridescent scales appear much brighter than

normal. He will vigorously and deliberately chase the female about, and when she finally halts abruptly, the actual mating may be imminent.

The spawning tank should be stocked with both abundant plant growth and a substratum of natural peat moss to facilitate nest building and the temperature gradually raised and maintained at between 82° and 86°F. In most cases, piranhas ready to spawn will do so without much preamble and without any special preparations on the part of the aquarist. If the tank is set up to the breeders' satisfaction and they have been adequately fed, a spawning may occur if the aquarium is large enough so that the fish may carry out their courtship and nest-building activities. The piranha is, incidentally, the only characin that constructs any sort of nest to receive the eggs—most charalins, with the exception of the bizarre splash tetra (*Copiena arnoldi*), scatter their eggs randomly in surrounding vegetation and leave them to their fate.

In a piranha spawning reported at the aquarium of the Zurich Zoological Park, the eggs were deposited in a large clump of Java moss and since it was impossible to

The bizarre splash tetra, *Copeina arnoldi,* jumps out of the water in ballet-like unison, depositing their eggs on a leaf. These small tetras get along with piranhas for some unknown reason. Photos by Jiri Palicka.

A young Serrasalmus rhombeus.

siphon the spawn from the tank, the moss and eggs were removed entirely and placed in a hatching tank with a temperature of 70°F. At the time, the eggs were being guarded by the male of the pair.

The fry hatched in four days and for several days thereafter remained suspended in the moss, later descending to the bottom of the tank where they remained randomly scattered on the substrate. At four days of age, the young fish began to feed on newly hatched brine shrimp, gradually moving up to copepods and daphnia. It was noted that even at that early stage of life, the fry were beginning to take an interest in each other and there was some squabbling and biting going on!

At the age of two months the largest of the fry were almost two inches in length and beginning to display the attractive, speckled pattern of the juvenile piranha. At the age of eight months, the young of this particular spawn had attained the length of five inches and had lost most of the juvenile pattern, being a pleasing shade of steel-blue and silver. On average, piranha fry will grow about one inch per month given adequate care and favorable tank conditions.

According to most reports of captive spawnings involving a group of breeders, the fish are quite rough with each other and injuries are common. Schulte reported that a lone male was discovered defending a particular spot in a large tank, and subsequent investigation revealed that a large spawn

An unidentified piranha collected and photographed by Dr. Herbert R. Axelrod in Guyana. This looks like the gentle kind of piranha and might make a community aquarium fish if more can be found.

had been deposited on the site. The guardian fish was badly injured about the head and flanks, but continued to vigorously defend the eggs against the other piranhas sharing the tank, though in spite of his best efforts, most of the eggs were eaten within 36 hours. Those few fry that hatched from the surviving eggs took refuge within the filter tank and were subsequently rescued and placed in a separate rearing tank. For the above and other reasons dealing with the jumpy, unpredictable nature of the parent fish, it is the better part of wisdom to remove either the adults or the eggs for rearing in a separate container if a high success rate of fry rearing is hoped for.

Many piranha species reportedly do practice some degree of brood care—usually on the part of the male parent, and unusual

This spotted *Metynnis lippincotianus* has the coloration of a juvenile *S. nattereri.*

Tank-raised
*Serrasalmus
nattereri* can
be kept
together if
they are
always well
fed. Photo by
I. Sazima.

for characins—but under captive conditions, the far better course is to hatch the eggs under controlled conditions. The space and general conditions conducive to fry-rearing that exist in the natural state are absent in the aquarium and thus the chances of reducing or eliminating altogether the stress that will cause parent fish to destroy their eggs or fry are chancy at best.

The rearing conditions reported for most of the successful hatchings of piranha eggs include a hatching temperature of 77°F, this raised to between 80 and 82°F after the fry have hatched. Considerable success has been had with a 50-50 distilled water/aged tankwater composition, with the tank treated with methyline blue to help prevent fungusing of the eggs. Aeration should be vigorous and filtration provided through glass wool and charcoal.

Hiroshi Azuma, renowned aquarist and breeder of rare and unusual fishes, successfully spawned the gold piranha (*S. gibbus*) for the

A very young,
2-inch-long
*Serrasalmus
hollandi.*
Photo by
Aaron
Norman.

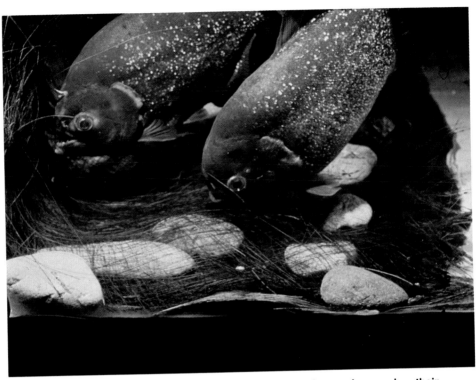

(Above) A breeding pair of *Serrasalmus nattereri* cleaning and preparing their spawning site. (Below) After selecting the site they spawn in atypical (abnormal) characin fashion laying their eggs in a glob and then guarding them! Photos by Hiroshi Azuma.

(Above) The spawning ritual is repeated again and again. (Below) A group of youngster all of which have chunks bitten out of their tails and dorsal fins. Photos by Azuma.

first time and his informative account of the event, published in the June, 1990 issue of *"Tropical Fish Hobbyist"* magazine, is certainly worth citing here.

Azuma set up a 220-gallon tank equipped with an abundance of plant growth and hiding places. The water was soft and slightly acid and maintained at between 80 – 84°F. The fish were three-year-old adults that were placed together and closely watched for signs of conflict. The female of this pair sustained considerable fin and body damage during the actual spawning activity, but healing was rapid and complete. The gold piranha is a species that apparently does not, in the captive environment at least, practice any brood care or protection of the eggs.

Azuma noted that once ready to spawn, "the female begins to fill with eggs, though her abdomen does not swell very much—perhaps only 1.2 to 1.3 times its normal size. The male's color darkens, somewhat, and the iridescent scales brighten, shining like diamonds. When you spot these subtle changes and think you have a pair, separate them and condition them on a variety of choice live foods, including plenty of feeder fishes.

"After a couple of weeks, a spawning attempt can be made. The male is placed in the spawning tank, and the female is added a day later. At this point, some males become excited immediately and may injure the female with their wild advances. But not all males act this way; some wait 10 days or more before spawning. Usually, if it's going to happen at all, spawning takes place by the 18th day after the breeders are placed together.

"Spawning begins in the late afternoon and continues for about three hours. The fish press close together near the bottom and the male curls his anal fin under the female's abdomen, presumably to better insure fertilization of the eggs.

"With my fish, I noted a very curious behavior: the male would cut off pieces of plants near the spawning site. At the time, the male had not spawned yet, and he did not eat the pieces of the plants he had cut. What this means, I do not know.

"Spawning will result in some 800-1200 eggs scattered randomly over the bottom. The fish do not care for their eggs in any way, so it is best to remove the parents when spawning is completed.

"At a temperature of 82°F, the eggs hatch in about 54 – 58 hours. A week later, the fry are free-swimming and can be fed live brine shrimp nauplii. Two weeks later they can also eat chopped tubifex and bloodworms. They grow very quickly, reaching an inch in length in only two months. At this point they begin to eat small live fishes, sometimes even their own kind, as is the case with other piranha species as well."

Growing young piranhas maintained in the captive environment should be provided with as much, if not more, room per fish than their elders. This requirement is due primarily to the fish's strongly cannibalistic nature, for at a very early age, piranha fry graduate to other small fishes as prey, and these may well be their siblings. As a good rule of thumb, young piranhas should be housed in no less than the standard "one gallon of water per one fish" formula often given for all fishes kept in aquaria, which would pretty much demand a tank of at the very least 55-gallons capacity for the very smallest fry. As they grow, they will have to be thinned and separated into roomy quarters that will continue to provide them with enough room to avoid each other and potential violent conspecific encounters. The end result of a successful spawning in which many fry are reared could well be a series of very large tanks housing six to ten young piranhas, all perpetually hungry and enjoying an uneasy truce with each other! The alternative, however, is simply letting the fish thin their own ranks, which the piranhas will most assuredly do, especially in the unnatural confines of an aquarium.

The hobbyist who enjoys success in spawning his fish is advised to swap the excess with other aquarists or a petshop, which might be willing to exchange healthy, young tank-reared piranhas for credit in live foods or equipment. But check first—normally, piranhas are fairly hot items in aquarium stores and always in demand, but as they can be difficult to maintain in an undamaged condition in crowded store display tanks, some dealers may be unwilling to accept them under any circumstances.

The Legal Aspect

Piranhas are high on the popularity roster with many aquarium hobbyists and a source of considerable interest and fascination for the public at large, but the group as a whole is not always held in the highest esteem by conservation and environmental authorities in the United States. The reasons for this official antipathy are several and complex, but in general it can be said that the very qualities that endear the piranha to hobbyists are those behind the dread fish and game officials feel when contemplating the consequences of the accidental or deliberate introduction of piranhas into temperate or subtropical waters.

The longterm effect of exotic species on an alien environment into which they have been introduced has been so well documented today that the pros and cons of the matter need not be covered in depth here. Though there have been some successes, notably the striped bass's transplantation to the West Coast, by and large, the overall effect of an exotic predator on the resident fauna is not a desirable one, to say the least. That the piranha is a predator, and an aggressive, relatively dangerous one, there is no doubt, but just how real is the threat that even one pair of piranha dumped into a lake in the South will quickly breed and fill that once benevolent body of water of water with bloodthirsty maneaters?

The answer is, it's practically nonexistent.

Piranhas are social creatures that, unlike such solitary predatory fishes as snakeheads or pikes, live and interact in schooling aggregations. The conditions required for spawning in their tropical home are complex and subtle and are rarely duplicated even in subtropical waters in this country, warm though a Florida slough may be. Even if a body of water approximating the piranha's native environment could be found in North America, determined and repeated introductions of many small piranhas would have to be made before the fish could even hope to establish a population of viable breeders. Most warmwater habitats in the southern United States are already populated with resident predators—large and smallmouth basses, pickerels, and snapping turtles, to name just three—which would quickly thin the ranks of the nervous, active, conspicuous piranhas introduced there. To larger predators, a small piranha is simply another potential food item! Just as in stocking a lake with desirable game fishes, all of the predators and competing species would have to be removed before a serious attempt was made to establish a self-sustaining population of piranhas.

The usual "piranha scares" trumpeted in the press are the result of one, or at the most two, adult piranhas being caught by a sport angler. These fish are almost always unwanted pet piranhas dumped into the lake or pond by a hobbyist who couldn't (or wouldn't) get rid of the creatures any other way, and although there is always the chance that a person could be bitten by such a piranha, that risk exists only when the successful fisherman is attempting to dehook his exotic catch. As noted before, that is precisely when the overwhelming majority of piranha "attacks" occur in the fish's home range!

The normal official reaction to such a piranha catch is one of over-reaction, especially if the incident has received much attention by the media. In most cases, the lake is treated with the fish-killing chemical Rotenone, destroying virtually all of the resident fishes, game or otherwise, but nary another piranha turns belly-up. In some cases, the authorities will electroshock the body of water if it is a smaller one, stunning but not killing the resident fishes, in order to asses the situation and determine if the bagged piranha is the only piranha present. In nearly all incidences, it is, and the reason is simple: in virtually all piranha scares, the lone culprit was an unwanted aquarium fish that was released there; any other "maneaters" in the lake exist only in the imagination and wishful thinking of those charged with eliminating the perceived threat.

Although laws regulating the sale or possession of piranhas may change as information regarding the piranha's inability to survive and reproduce itself in temperate waters comes to the attention of fish and game authorities, it can be stated that most of the extreme southern states prohibit the keeping of Serrasalmids by private individuals. Such legislative control does not, however, always follow a logical pattern, as two northern states—Connecticut and Minnesota—also forbid the sale and ownership of piranhas. The idea of a piranha surviving a Minnesota winter is fanciful, to say the least, and makes one wonder whether anyone remotely resembling an ichthyologist was consulted when the law was written!

Few, if any, piranhas are sold illegally on the retail level in states where they are prohibited—it's simply not worth the risk to the reputable petshop—but many find their way into private hands via illicit smuggling or innocent transport or fish swaps between hobbyists in one state to those in another. But whatever the source of acquisition, no piranha owner should ever discard an unwanted fish anywhere in waters outside the natural range, period. This is much less in concern for the supposed threat to humans than from the aspect of cruelty to the piranha itself, for a piranha "liberated" in temperate waters is surely doomed to starvation or slowly freezing to death with the onset of fall weather.

Serrasalmus notatus. Photo by Drs. Leo G. Nico and Donald C. Taphorn.

The Piranha Keeper's Code of Conduct

Because of its many positive attribute and, to no small degree, its aura of mystery spiced with just a hint of menace the piranha has rather suddenly become enormously popular as a pet in many western nations. The dictionary defines the word "pet" variously as "any domesticated or tamed animal that is kept as a favorite and cared for affectionately," or, "to fondle or caress." The piranha quite conceivably falls within the bounds of the first definition, but would surely not welcome the nature of the attention implied in the latter.

In the end, it requires a considerable stretch of the imagination to call a piranha (or nearly any other fish) a pet, at least within the accepted sense of the word. In fact, the piranha is a wild animal that accepts captivity more or less gracefully if its requirements are met and the man-made environment is to its liking. Under those circumstances, the fish will provide its keeper with an experience that is as close to that of a pet relationship as you're likely to see in fishes, for the serrasalmids are "brighter" than many other fishes and respond quickly to stimuli, objects, and people they encounter in or near their surroundings.

The one single factor that sets the piranha apart from most other fishes that might be considered for the status of pethood is the overstated but nonetheless very real element of danger. A large oscar may well bite if it mistakes its owner's fingers for a food offering or is defending a spawn in its tank. But no one seriously anticipates a trip to the hospital as the result, for an oscar (or any other cichlid, for that matter) is not equipped for the kind of aggressive, killing attack a piranha is designed for and fully capable of. Anyone bitten by a large piranha will long remember the occasion and sustain a wound that is not to be sneezed at.

In view of the risk, no matter how small, inherent in the keeping of piranhas in the home aquarium, we offer an aquarists' Code of Conduct that, it is hoped, will help you derive the most enjoyment from what can and should be a long and pleasant relationship with your "pet" piranha:

*Know your piranha. It is hoped that this book will inspire the interested reader to progress further on the subject of the piranha and its nature and environment. Only by thoroughly familiarizing yourself with the animal you have taken personal responsibility for, will the experience by a rewarding one—both to you, and to the piranha. There are many fine books and periodicals available today that cover the subject of piranhas in depth, and on both the popular and scientific level.

*Handle with care. A piranha may be "only a fish," but it is a predator that is fully capable of inflicting injury if handled recklessly. For this reason, the aquarist seeking to impress friends shouldn't—

not with a piranha! Never take foolish liberties with a large specimen under the blissful assumption that "the fish knows me ." This is looking for trouble.

*Treat it with respect. Too many piranhas are purchased solely as an object of novelty. Most people today are well aware of the fish's reputation for ferocity and aggressiveness and some are intrigued by the idea of keeping a potentially dangerous animal in their home. This is the wrong reason to bring a piranha into your home for it serves to render a living creature into an object of fear and even revulsion among uniformed people—not the message you wish to deliver in this environmentally aware age!

*Time to part company? Sooner or later the time will arrive when you will have to consider disposing of your piranha, one way or the other. Piranhas will live for many years in a large aquarium if well cared for and many aquarists keep their fish for life, so to speak, and never arrive at that time when they must find another home for them. For the average hobbyist, the end of the relationship comes either through the unfortunate demise of the piranha, or the sudden need, such as a relocation or a departure from fishkeeping, to dispose of the fish. Whatever the case, as noted above, an unwanted piranha SHOULD NOT be released in waters anywhere outside its nature range, regardless of whether it could conceivably survive there or not. Public aquariums sometimes accept piranhas from private aquarists, except those in states where possession of the fish is illegal. One should always contact a public aquarium first, before showing up with any large, unwanted fish in a plastic bag!

Membership in a local aquarium club is always a good idea under any circumstances, and it may reap dividends when you're stuck with that oversized piranha. In many cases, a fellow hobbyist who simply has to have that beautiful creature you wish to get rid of will materialize out of the woodwork if you advertise in a club publication.

Petshops MAY be willing to take an unwanted piranha off your hands, especially if your purchased it there. Most shops offer a credit against foods or equipment, or will swap the fish for another species, but, as with public aquariums, call first and ask.

IN SUM

Over the past few decades, the life of the average person in the world's industrialized nations has become both complex and rather mundane in its daily progression, so that, increasingly, people tend to seek out the strange and the exotic to add a bit of spice to life. In the area of pets, creatures are being kept in private homes today that never would have been considered "pets" in any sense of the word not all that long ago. Tarantulas, walking stick insects, many species of reptiles, land hermit crabs, ocelots, and armadillos, to name just a few, are among the many "exotics" that have found favor with people looking for something beyond the traditional dog, cat, and goldfish. The piranha is also one of these exotic newcomers to the pet scene and as such has found a ready and willing following of admirers. The reason for this interest, as noted earlier, stems from the piranha's dual image of mystery and menace, for most of the known species are neither very large nor very spectacular in form and color. It is the piranha's potential for inflicting injury that is, in part, behind its allure for the average person, even he or she contemplating a fish for the living room aquarium.

In recent years, another, perhaps much more important and critical reason for learning more about piranhas has emerged—the rampant destruction of the fish's habitat. When people conjure up images of vast and impenetrable rainforests, they usually think of such familiar animals as monkeys, parrots, and the big cats as typically attendant wildlife, and perhaps no other fish comes to mind more readily as a "jungle animal" than the piranha.

Piranhas are indeed true rainforest creatures whose physical requirements are met by the unique and fragile ecology offered by that marvelous environment. The neotropical forests are today being hacked down at a fearful rate, and when they have all been converted into cattle pastures and human housing, their unique wildlife, numbering in the thousands of species, will have vanished with them. This dismal future surely awaits most, if not all the known piranha species unless international action is taken mmediately to stem this environmental havoc.

To fully understand the life history of the piranhas is to come to appreciate its value as a small but integral part of the entire ecosphere of the Neotropics. With understanding will come the inevitable unravelling of most of the stuff and nonsense surrounding these fishes, but in their place will be instituted a compassion and committment that will be an absolutely indispensible weapon in the fight to save the remnants of the piranha's jungle home.

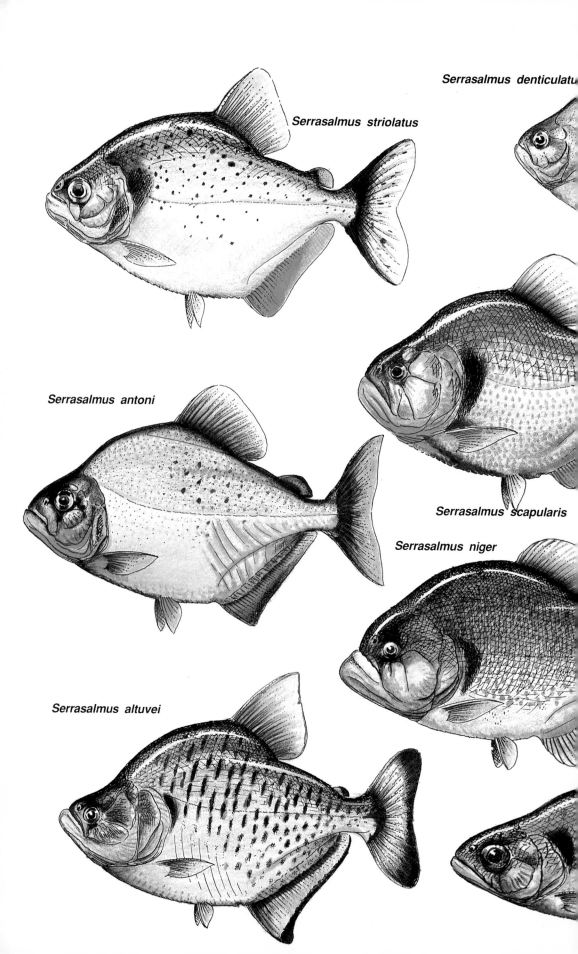

Serrasalmus denticulatu

Serrasalmus striolatus

Serrasalmus antoni

Serrasalmus scapularis

Serrasalmus niger

Serrasalmus altuvei

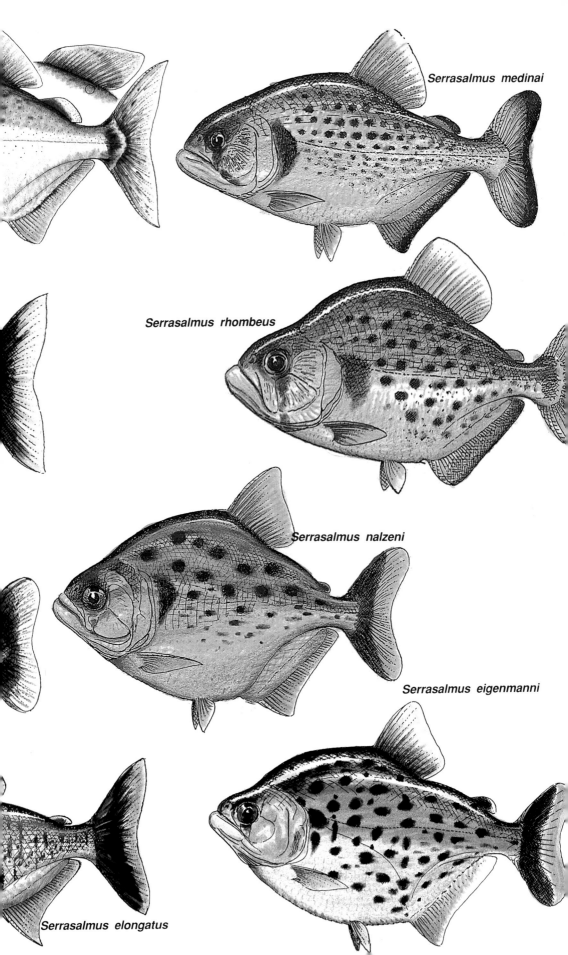

Serrasalmus medinai

Serrasalmus rhombeus

Serrasalmus nalzeni

Serrasalmus eigenmanni

Serrasalmus elongatus

Index